PANTRY COCKTAILS

INVENTIVE SIPS FROM EVERYDAY STAPLES
(and a few nibbles too)

KATHERINE COBBS

TILLER PRESS

New York   London   Toronto   Sydney   New Delhi

TILLER PRESS

An Imprint of Simon & Schuster, Inc.
1230 Avenue of the Americas
New York, NY 10020

First Tiller Press hardcover edition May 2021

TILLER PRESS and colophon are trademarks of Simon & Schuster, Inc.

For information about special discounts for bulk purchases, please contact
Simon & Schuster Special Sales at 1-866-506-1949 or business@simonandschuster.com.

The Simon & Schuster Speakers Bureau can bring authors to your live event.
For more information or to book an event, contact the Simon & Schuster Speakers Bureau
at 1-866-248-3049 or visit our website at www.simonspeakers.com.

Cover and interior design by Matt Ryan
Illustrations by Maya Metz Logue
Conceived and produced by Blueline Creative Group LLC
Visit: bluelinecreativegroup.com
Concept, copy, and recipes by Katherine Cobbs
Recipe testing by Rebecca Withers and Carlos Briceño

Manufactured in the United States of America

10 9 8 7 6 5 4 3 2 1

Library of Congress Cataloging-in-Publication Data has been applied for.

ISBN 978-1-9821-6762-2
ISBN 978-1-9821-6763-9 (ebook)

I raise my glass to all who hunkered down, stayed home, and got innovative in the ways they worked, lived, connected, and cooked when it mattered most . . . and that made all the difference.

To my three daughters—Parker, Ella, and Addie—it was a rare joy having you all under our roof again, and I am grateful for that silver lining. Cheers!

TABLE
of
CONTENTS

Introduction

Growing up in the '70s and '80s, my big sister, Rebecca, and I would play what we called "The Tasting Game," an exciting, mysterious, and quite often disgusting game that I prided myself on being really skilled at. We each took turns being blindfolded while the other went to the kitchen to find the weirdest ingredient or combination of ingredients for the other to taste and attempt to identify. The prize was in just getting it right. "Worcestershire on a Nutter Butter!" or "mashed banana with malt vinegar!" My mom was never thrilled to find bouillon cubes with missing corners or the Baker's chocolate with teeth marks, but the game certainly helped me hone my taste buds.

Other than being human food (a rule implemented after the time my sister fed me a piece of a Gaines-burgers dog food patty), there were no rules about what ingredients could be combined and offered. If I wanted to stir oil from a can of Nova Scotia sardines with mango chutney from India and feed it to my sister on a piece of stale Melba toast while she sat on a lawn chair in our Oklahoma backyard, she might be thoroughly grossed out, but it was all in the name of experimentation and fun.

Fast-forward to my culinary school days years later, when food television was in its infancy and shows like *Chopped* and *Iron Chef* had yet to hit the airways. Exam days at Tante Marie's Cooking School in the North Beach neighborhood of San Francisco meant each of my dozen classmates got a sheet pan of random ingredients. We had to prepare a dish using the assortment of ingredients that we were given, and the techniques we recently had learned, and then serve our creation at a specified time to a panel of judges that included our culinary instructor; the school's owner, Mary Risley; and an outside expert or two. Quite regularly big-name chefs or notable cookbook authors like Madeleine Kamman or Nick Malgieri were among the visiting guest judges. No matter who was on the tasting panel, our task was always intimidating . . . but also exciting, mysterious, and creative. In many ways, it felt as though I'd come full circle, only this tasting game was about making disparate ingredients harmonize as deliciously as possible to impress the judges.

At one point or another in all of our lives, we have faced a similar scenario that has us playing kitchen MacGyver, whipping up a magnificent meal or a delicious appetizer from the odds and ends of the pantry or fridge. It took a pandemic to get many of us to realize just how creative we could be with the ingredients that we had on hand. That same improvisational approach is easily applied to home bartending, too. Understanding how to enlist the condiments, jams, pickles, and sauces cluttering up your cabinets and refrigerator means you can craft inventive, flavorful cocktails on the fly to satisfy a craving, reinvent a drink from a beloved watering hole, or express your creativity by using what you have at your fingertips in order to avoid an expensive outing to the market and liquor store. With a few key spirits, cupboard staples, or an assortment of treasures from your windowsill, garden, or fridge, you can whip up outstanding cocktails guaranteed to satisfy and impress. Surely, that's worth raising a glass to!

—Katherine Cobbs

The Cocktail Hour Kitchen

Countless books and online guides tell you how to stock the bar and kitchen, but when push comes to shove, or a virus leads to quarantine, sometimes you are forced to get scrappy and creative with what you have on hand. (I cannot begin to count how many times I've been in a hotel room where no wine opener is to be found!) And because desperate times call for desperate measures, I always find a way.

More than once, my exhausted family has arrived at a vacation rental long after stores and restaurants have closed, and yet we manage to cobble together a decent meal from what's in our cooler and the random spices and condiments left behind by previous renters. Through trial and error and lots of improvisation you just learn what works together and what mash-ups are best to avoid. Sometimes you just might be surprised to find that what you end up with is actually better than what you were after.

Did you know that you can make a damn good Manhattan sans orange bitters or sweet vermouth using muddled charred orange peel and a splash of white grape juice from your kid's juice box stash? Yes, you can! It's a worthy approximation that is sublime and satisfying, and it doesn't involve an investment in two bottles you may only rarely use. Bourbon is mandatory, of course!

As much as I love improvising with ingredients, I've always been a fan of kitchen hacks, too—using the spout end of a funnel to pit a cherry, getting crushed ice by smashing ice cubes in a zip-top bag with a cast-iron skillet, freezing citrus wheels or berries to add to drinks to keep them cool without diluting, and so on.

No cocktail shaker? Enlist a mason jar or water bottle instead. The blender bottle with a ball whisk used to mix protein powder drinks is another great shaker option in some instances. Lack a muddler? A wooden spoon or the pusher stick for your blender work wonders. Looking for a swizzle stick or barspoon? Turn to a long-handled, iced-tea spoon or chopstick to do the trick.

When you don't have the exact ingredient or tool called for and yet you figure out how to re-create what you crave, it's empowering. You might be surprised to find that when your cupboard and fridge are almost bare and you really do need to make that grocery store run, you test yourself by holding off just one more day to see just what sort of MacGyver magic you can whip up.

It's become routine at my house that when we're faced with the odds and ends of an almost-empty fridge and are too lazy to head to the market, we pull together a food board for an easy pickup meal. Arranged beautifully, it feels elaborate and festive and it's a fun thing to gather around. Stale bread can be brushed with olive oil and toasted and then rubbed with a garlic clove for easy crostini. Leftover bits of cheese from the cheese drawer can be combined in the food processor with a sprinkle of white wine from the fridge and fresh herbs from the window box to create what the French call *fromage fort* (*see* page 134). Pair that with cut-up fruit and vegetables arranged artfully. Add nuts, olives, pickles, and some dried fruit for more interest and texture. And voilà! Like loaves and fishes, where there seemed to be nothing much left, an abundant spread appears. Cheers to that!

The Liquor Cabinet

While I am all for improvising when it comes to cooking and mixing cocktails, for the backbone of spirited drinks—the liquor—there are no cheats. Until someone shares a hack showing how to replicate all the flavorful and heady aspects of an aged whiskey on the fly in minutes, a trip to the liquor store to stock up will remain a necessity.

Start your list by thinking about what you like, what you prefer to drink most often at home, and what you order at a bar when out. I enjoy sipping mezcal or bourbon straight more than in mixed drinks, while I prefer vodka, rum, and gin in cocktails to sipping solo. If a Negroni is your go-to cocktail, then definitely add a bottle of Campari and sweet vermouth to the gin on your list. Once you identify what you enjoy, let your budget and interest inspire you. Stock up on a couple of different bottles or start a robust collection that allows you to explore the nuances of a particular spirit and how it plays alone and with other ingredients.

I try to keep at least one bottle from each of the categories of essential spirits below stocked in my home bar. With a bottle from each category, plus a couple of liqueurs, I can make most any cocktail, and certainly fill the requests of friends and houseguests. If you don't entertain or only drink vodka, then that simplifies your liquor cabinet list tremendously.

The cocktails and mixed drinks, which I also refer to as "cocktails," in this book use spirits primarily from the categories below. There are numerous offerings within each category—varied brands, styles, and variations. Start with a bottle or two from each category to build your home bar.

Agave Spirits	**Rum**
Brandy	**Vodka**
Gin	**Whiskey**

The additional bottles that you can add to your inventory are practically infinite, and new ones continuously come to market—from a mother lode of lovely liqueurs to a bevy of bracing bitters, sweet syrups, and seltzers, sodas, tonics, ales, and juices, plus wine, including fortified and aromatized varieties. If a liqueur or mixer is critical to a recipe in this book, it is listed in the ingredients. I suggest a suitable "Sneaky Cheat" whenever possible to mimic flavors using everyday ingredients that you are more likely to have on hand.

Dashes, Doses & Rim Gracers

A dash of this, a drop of that . . . sometimes it's the little things that take a drink from ho hum to HELLO! A classic 3-2-1 margarita made with 3 parts tequila, 2 parts orange liqueur, and 1 part lime juice is tart and refreshing at its most basic, but a tiny pinch of salt added to the shaker accentuates the interplay of sour and sweet in a noticeable way. A splash of watermelon cordial or a chili-lime rim salt are the cocktail accent equivalents of the cool shades or striking shoes that make a tasteful outfit. Master basic recipes for a few key add-ins and you can create numerous drink variations using everyday ingredients that you likely have on hand to complement whatever cocktail you're crafting.

SUBLIME SYRUPS

You can sweeten a tipple with agave syrup, honey, maple syrup, corn syrup, cane syrup, sorghum, molasses, or any other sweet syrup, but must consider how the distinctive flavor of each will work with the other ingredients you are using. The neutral sweetener most often enlisted in mixology is simple syrup, a blend of sugar and water. The standard recipe is a 1:1 ratio that is shaken, blended, or heated over low heat until the sugar fully dissolves. Heated versions keep longer than shaken or blended versions. Rich simple syrups with a higher 2:1 ratio of sugar to water also last longer. To really extend the life of a large batch of simple syrup, add a neutral high-proof alcohol and it will keep in the fridge for a couple months.

SIMPLE SYRUP: Combine 1 cup sugar and 1 cup water in a saucepan over low heat. Stir until the sugar dissolves. Remove from heat to cool. (Alternatively, shake the sugar and water in a sealed container or whirl in a high-speed blender until the sugar dissolves.) Stir in ½ ounce overproof vodka. Transfer the syrup to a clean bottle and refrigerate for up to 2 months. **Makes about 1¾ cups.**

RICH SIMPLE SYRUP: Combine 1 cup sugar to ½ cup water and follow the directions above. **Makes about 1¼ cups.**

Flavored Simple Syrup is infused with spices, herbs, or aromatics like ginger, lemongrass, vanilla bean, apple peels, pear peels, and dried flowers. These ingredients can be steeped in water to make a "tea" that is used to make the flavored simple syrup, or they may be added to the syrup to infuse it with flavor as it cools. Flavored syrups used in this book are included with the cocktail recipes into which they are mixed.

HONEY SYRUP: Mix 1 cup honey with ½ cup water in a bottle or jar. Secure the lid and shake vigorously to combine. Refrigerate for up to 2 months. **Makes about 1½ cups.**

CITRUS OLEO SACCHARUM: Citrus oleo saccharum translates to "citrus sugar oil" and is made when the oils extracted from citrus peels dissolve into sugar. Use organic fruit and be sure to remove any wax on the surface of the skins so that their natural oils can escape. Use a vegetable peeler to remove all the peels (avoiding pith) from lemons, limes, tangerines, oranges, grapefruits, or use a mix of citrus peel varieties. Layer 1 cup of citrus zest strips with 1 cup superfine sugar in a jar and muddle well. Secure the lid and leave the jar at room temperature for at least 12 hours and up to 24 hours, shaking often, until the sugar has dissolved. Strain the syrup and store it in the refrigerator for up to 1 week. **Makes about ¾ cup.**

FRUIT CORDIAL: Combine 1 cup sugar and 1½ cups frozen or fresh fruit that has been peeled and seeded, if necessary, in a saucepan over medium heat until the sugar melts and the fruit breaks down. Reduce heat to low and simmer until the fruit is very soft, 20 to 30 minutes. Remove from heat. Strain through a fine-mesh strainer, pressing the solids with the back of a spoon. Let cool. Strain again. Add ½ ounce overproof vodka. Transfer to a bottle and refrigerate for up to 1 month. **Makes ¾ to 1 cup.**

GRENADINE: Follow the recipe for Simple Syrup (above) using pure pomegranate juice in place of the water. Add ½ teaspoon orange flower with the overproof vodka and transfer to a bottle. Refrigerate for up to 1 month. (This method may be used with other fruit juices to make an array of fruit syrups.) **Makes about 1½ cups.**

RIM GRACERS

A savory or sweet rim is a nice embellishment to the glass for many cocktails. Dampen the rim of a glass and dip it in a layer of salt or sugar alone or mixed with other ingredients, such as grated zest, ground spices, sweet or savory crumbs, and minced herbs. Consider rimming just half the glass so that the drink can be savored on its own, too. Rim salts and sugars used in this book accompany the recipes where they are a suggested garnish. Most recipes make enough to rim 2 to 3 glasses.

SNEAKY TIKI CHEATS

Two classic tiki mixers are nutty orgeat, a cloudy almond syrup scented with orange and rose that adds a distinctive note to Mai Tais and Scorpion cocktails, and falernum, an almond syrup infused with warm spices and aromatics that is a classic component of the Zombie and Rum Swizzle cocktails. The recipes below are quick substitutions for the real thing. Don't limit the use of these to tiki drinks alone. The nutty, warm spice-meets-citrus flavors of both pair surprisingly well with whiskey, brandy, and even gin.

Cheater's Orgeat: Make Simple Syrup using 1 cup sugar and 1 cup almond milk in place of the usual water. Add 1 teaspoon almond extract, ½ teaspoon orange flower water, and ½ teaspoon rose flower water. Add ½ ounce overproof vodka. Transfer to a bottle and store in the refrigerator for up to 1 month. **Makes 1¾ cups.**

Cheater's Falernum: Make Cheater's Orgeat, adding the finely grated zest of 1 lime, 1 tablespoon grated fresh ginger root, ⅛ teaspoon ground cloves, ⅛ teaspoon ground allspice, and ⅛ teaspoon ground nutmeg and steep for 20 minutes over low heat. Remove from heat and cool completely. Refrigerate for 24 hours and then strain through a fine-mesh strainer. Add ½ ounce overproof vodka. Transfer to a bottle and keep refrigerated for up to 1 month. **Makes about 1½ cups.**

THE BITTER TRUTH

The choices for concentrated alcoholic cocktail and digestive bitters on the market are abundant. Each lends a distinctive note to drinks while buffering sweetness or taming tartness with a unique astringent profile. Traditionally, bitters were sipped alone or added to stirred cocktails, but today anything goes. If you love an Old Fashioned, then a bottle of Angostura bitters is a must in your liquor cabinet. If a Sazerac is your usual, having Peychaud's on hand is key for making a classic one at home. A wealth of recipes for homemade bitters exist in books and online. Most take weeks to make and require obscure ingredients like gentian root, cinchona bark, or horehound. It's easiest to stock up on the bottles of bitters you'll use most. Bittermens, Scrappy's, Fee Brothers, El Guapo, and Jack Rudy are among a handful of readily available brands that offer any array of flavors and styles.

THINK TWICE ABOUT ICE

Fresh, clear ice is key to great mixed drinks. If the ice in your freezer's ice maker bin has been around for a while, it's likely taken on off-flavors or become cloudy. Toss it so that the machine makes new ice. Alternatively, fill ice trays with filtered water and pop out the ice and store in freezer bags as soon as it's frozen rock solid. Your drinks will look and taste better!

THE FRIDGE

1

Never underestimate the bounty of ingredients inside your fridge that can be shaken and strained or stirred into cocktails that explode with flavor. Consider all those last drips and drops in condiment bottles, jam jars, syrup jugs, and so forth as the home mixologist's medium for infusing drinks with interest and complexity. Adding olive brine to a martini may be commonplace, but why not incorporate pickle juice into your gimlet or Korean gochujang paste into a poolside Michelada? Having a party? Let guests in on the action with a jam jar cocktail bar. They can make their own jammy cocktails to shake and drink straight from the jars. Let the ingredients you have on hand inspire and guide you. The caramelly sweet notes of bourbon pair beautifully with apple, so try adding a spoonful of apple butter and a sprig of rosemary to bourbon in a cocktail shaker for juicy spin on a Manhattan (see page 30) that tastes more upstate apple orchard than buttoned-up Big Apple. We don't think twice about experimenting and improvising when it comes to cooking, so it's time to show that same creative courage when crafting cocktails at home.

Condiment Cocktails

Condiments are flavor bombs that can add a sweet, salty, sour, earthy, or complex burst of tasty interest to an array of dishes. One way to discern how a condiment might work in a cocktail is to think about the many ways you put it to use with food and then consider where you might substitute it for ingredients commonly used in cocktails that have a similar flavor profile. The thought process might go something like this: Mustard is a great emulsifier in a vinaigrette, so maybe it could serve a similar function in a drink where an egg white or aquafaba is typically added for body. Since mustard can have the sinus-tingling quality of horseradish, a squirt in a Bloody Mary might be delicious or could take the place of hot sauce in a Michelada. On that note, maybe a new spin on the Mary using clear Tomato Water (*see* page 74) and mustard seed–infused vodka could usher in a sunny new brunch trend. Because mustard is so distinctive and bold, it is important to combine it with other strong flavors like the spiced rum found in the Captain Mustard Sour (*see* page 21). Remember, the fridge is your oyster and the wonders to be found under all those caps and lids are just another medium in the home mixologist's palette for making provocative sips to quench any craving.

SUSHI MARY

SERVES 4   This mouthwatering Mary borrows from fridge, cupboard, spice drawer, and garden for a riff bursting with umami, sip after sip. White miso paste adds the earthy savoriness that Worcestershire traditionally brings. Crushed coriander seeds stand in for celery seeds and wasabi for horseradish, while lots of fresh lemon juice lends the expected tantalizing tartness. A dose of the sweet brine from a jar of pickled ginger adds something altogether welcome and new as does the addition of sake (though you may use just vodka if you prefer). For a nice contrast, rim one side of the glass with furikake seasoning, a Japanese spice blend traditionally sprinkled on rice.

Furikake seasoning (optional)

Lemon slice

½ **teaspoon coriander seeds, crushed**

½ **teaspoon white miso paste**

½ **to 1 teaspoon prepared wasabi paste**

1 **ounce pickled ginger juice**

1 **ounce fresh lemon juice**

1 **ounce vodka**

1 **ounce honjozo sake**

6 **ounces tomato juice, such as Clamato**

Hot sauce

Lemon wedge

Cucumber ribbon

Daikon ribbon

Pickled ginger

Rim a highball glass with furikake seasoning, if desired. Drop a lemon slice in the bottom of the glass. In a small bowl, mix the crushed coriander seeds, miso and wasabi pastes, and ginger and lemon juices. Stir well to combine. Pour into the prepared glass. Add the vodka, sake, tomato juice, and hot sauce. Add ice and stir well to chill. Garnish with a lemon wedge. Thread the cucumber, daikon, and pickled ginger on a bamboo skewer and rest the skewer across the rim of the glass.

PANTRY GEM

Eden Shake furikake seasoning is a sesame and sea vegetable blend made without starches and fillers, simply from seaweed flakes, sea salt, black and white sesame seeds, and shiso leaves that were pickled in ume plum vinegar before being dehydrated and crushed. Use it to season rice, grilled fish, dress up a scoop of cottage cheese, stir into Greek yogurt for a quick creamy dip, or add a few shakes to a piping-hot bowl of miso soup.

NOTE: If you're allergic to shellfish or sensitive to MSG, a purified form of natural glutamate, substitute a tomato juice of your preference. I love the umami notes that Clamato adds here.

GOCHUJANG MICHELADA

SERVES 1   If you like the sparkly and spicy flavors of a classic Michelada, you will swoon over this spin that incorporates gochujang, the Korean fermented red chile, soybean, and sticky rice paste that is packed with meaty umami flavor. Just a touch of the paste adds a savoriness that keeps you salivating and sipping.

2 teaspoons kosher salt

2 teaspoons gochugaru chile flakes (*see* Pantry Gem *below*)

2 teaspoons lime zest

Lime wedge

½ to 1 ounce Michelada Mix (*recipe follows*)

1 ounce freshly squeezed lime juice

1 (12-ounce) bottle ice-cold light beer

Lime wheel

First make the Gochugaru-Lime Rim Salt: Combine the kosher salt, gochugaru chile flakes, and lime zest on a saucer. Rub the lip of a pilsner or pint glass with a lime wedge. Invert the glass on the saucer and twist to coat the rim. This makes enough for 2 to 3 drinks.

Add the Michelada Mix and lime juice to the glass. Fill with ice and top with the beer. Serve with a lime wheel and the bottle of remaining beer alongside for topping off.

MICHELADA MIX

Slowly whisk 5 ounces freshly squeezed lime juice with 3 tablespoons gochujang paste in a bowl to blend. Add 4 ounces Frank's RedHot sauce and 2 tablespoons soy sauce, and whisk to thoroughly combine. Store in a lidded jar in the refrigerator up to 1 month. **Makes about 1¾ cups.**

PANTRY GEM

Seek out Mother In Law's Gochugaru Korean Chile Flakes in the spice aisle or global aisle of most supermarkets, or find it online. Use it as a seasoning for grilled meats and seafood, as you would red chili flakes on pizza or pasta, and sprinkle on popcorn.

SQUIRT BOTTLE SOURS

Tart and refreshing, the bright acidity of sour cocktails is irresistible. Here, a classic variation on the Daisy—or margarita—gets a dose of zesty heat from a squirt of sriracha and is lengthened with soda for a tantalizing tingle. In another condiment concoction, a squeeze of Dijon lends body in a sour cocktail where an egg white typically would, plus it melds beautifully with the honey, lemon, nutty orgeat, burnt orange peel, and spiced rum—a medley that would make a fine marinade for meat, too. Oil and water may not mix, but in this final variation, a judicious dose of toasted sesame oil elevates a frothy gin sour spiked with a spurt of tamarind puree and lots of lime juice for far-flung juicy flavor sip after sublime sip.

SRIRACHA MUCHACHA
SESAME STREET SOUR
CAPTAIN MUSTARD SOUR

SRIRACHA MUCHACHA

SERVES 1 Garlicky sriracha has become as commonplace as Louisiana hot pepper sauce. Sure, it's delicious in a Bloody Mary or Michelada, but it's also pretty divine in a smoky mezcal cocktail like this mouthwatering Daisy. If you have it prepared, use 1 ounce mixed Citrus Oleo Saccharum (*see* page 7) in place of the liqueur and agave nectar. Jicama can be peeled, sliced, and cut into a variety of shapes for a nice, crisp garnish. Use cookie or aspic cutters to create fun shapes.

2 ounces mezcal or sotol

1 ounce freshly squeezed lime juice

½ ounce orange liqueur

½ ounce agave nectar

½ ounce sriracha sauce

Seltzer or club soda

Lime wedge

Peeled jicama star

Combine the mezcal or sotol, lime juice, liqueur, agave nectar, and sriracha in a shaker with ice. Shake vigorously and strain over fresh ice in a double old-fashioned glass. Top with soda water and garnish with a lime wedge and a jicama star.

SNEAKY CHEAT
Substitute an equal amount of frozen orange juice concentrate for orange liqueur in most recipes. Add a drop of orange extract to really drive home the complex orange flavor.

SESAME STREET SOUR

SERVES 1 Heady and tart with a distinctive hit of toasted sesame seeds, this is a full-bodied sour to enjoy slowly. The first sip conjures a cold noodle bowl in the best of ways, but as the drink warms, the tartness of the tamarind and the aroma of mint bloom. For a more pronounced minty note, clap a sprig between your palms and add it to the cocktail shaker at the start.

2 ounces London Dry Gin

1 ounce freshly squeezed lime juice

½ ounce tamarind puree

½ ounce Simple Syrup (*see* page 6)

¼ teaspoon toasted sesame oil

1 large egg white

Fresh mint sprig

Cucumber spear

Toasted white and black sesame seeds (optional)

Combine the gin, lime juice, tamarind puree, simple syrup, sesame oil, and egg white in a shaker; dry shake for 30 seconds. Add ice and shake for 30 seconds more. Double strain into a coupe glass. Add a mint sprig and cucumber spear. Sprinkle the surface with toasted sesame seeds, if desired.

TIP: Add the egg white to the shaker last to minimize the time it sits with the acidic ingredients, so there is less worry about coagulation or a change in texture.

PANTRY GEM
While researching my book *Tequila & Tacos*, a bartender showed me the squeeze bottle of Tamicon Organic Tamarind Concentrate he kept behind the bar. The convenient packaging makes it ideal for adding the perfect dose to sauces, seltzer, and cocktails. Find it online or at ethnic markets.

CAPTAIN MUSTARD SOUR

SERVES 1 When Captain Morgan's spiced rum and Dijon mustard collide with citrus, honey, almond, and ample fizz, you get this savory-and-spice sour cocktail. While it's not for everyone, mustard has been making an appearance in cocktails for a while now. Its emulsification properties act much like an egg white in sours, lending body to the drink. The mustard flavor is super subtle, but it harmonizes well with all the other players.

- 1½ ounces Captain Morgan's spiced rum
- ¼ ounce orgeat or Cheater's Orgeat (*see* page 8)
- ½ ounce freshly squeezed lemon juice
- ½ ounce Honey Syrup (*see* page 7)
- ¼ Dijon mustard
- Club soda
- 2 orange peel coins (optional)
- Orange wheel

Combine the rum, orgeat, lemon juice, honey syrup, and mustard in a shaker with ice. Shake vigorously and strain into an ice-filled Collins glass. Top with soda water.

If desired, hold a coin-size piece of orange peel over the glass between your finger and thumb with the zest side facing toward the surface of the drink. Hold the flame of a match or lighter an inch from the zest as you squeeze it to express and flame the citrus oils over the drink. Drop the peel in the glass. Repeat with the other coin of orange peel.

Garnish with an orange wheel.

PANTRY GEM

Club soda, seltzer, and sparkling water are interchangeable in cocktails, but club soda is worth keeping in your pantry. Both club soda and seltzer are carbonated in the factory, while sparkling water is naturally carbonated. Unlike seltzer, club soda has minerals added—typically sodium bicarbonate, sodium chloride, disodium phosphate, or potassium sulfate. These additives may boost the bubbly's stain-fighting abilities. Sip club soda to soothe an upset tummy and neutralize acid. Water houseplants with it to boost their growth. Add it to pancake, waffle or cake batters, and even to beaten eggs for an omelet with added fluffiness.

THE VILLAGE PUB BOARD

After college, I lived in DC for a stretch, and my friends and I frequented a basement tavern called the Brickskeller. It was an easy gathering place for friends coming from jobs on Capitol Hill, Georgetown, and Dupont Circle. We tried to work our way through a menu of thousands of beers (though we barely made a dent), and always ordered several cheese and charcuterie boards to share at the table. It was an economical way to stuff ourselves as we sipped. This food board pays tribute to that place with a sampling of great pub-inspired fare you might find stateside and beyond.

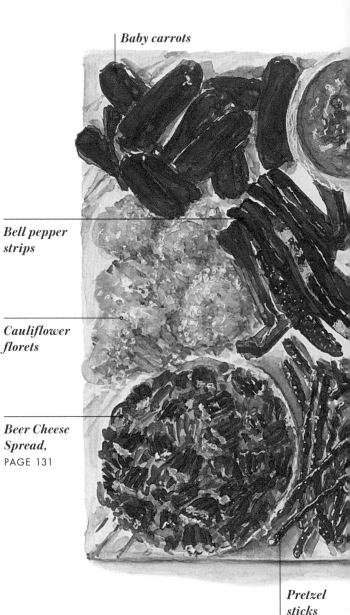

Baby carrots

Bell pepper strips

Cauliflower florets

Beer Cheese Spread, PAGE 131

Pretzel sticks

Russian Dressing, PAGE 135

Reubens-in-a-Blanket, PAGE 151

Grainy mustard

Bread & butter pickles

Brat Tots, PAGE 145

Salt-roasted peanuts in the shell

Jam & Syrup Cocktails

When presented with the last spoonful at the bottom of a jar of preserves or the remaining few drips of honey or maple syrup in the bottle, consider it an opportunity to get crafty. There are so many inventive ways to make sure that these sweet refrigerator staples are good to the last drop: Toss a minced shallot, splash of champagne vinegar, salt, pepper, and olive oil into the dregs of a jar of strawberry jam and shake it up to create a mouthwatering fruity vinaigrette. Spread that last scoop of jam or squirt of honey over a log of goat cheese for an easy appetizer. Muddle the last of the maple syrup with lemon wedges and thyme in the bottom of a mason jar, add bourbon, brewed black tea, and ice for a boozy Bourbon-Maple Sweet Tea Thyme (*see* page 27) that might have become the late Arnold Palmer's new post-tee tipple. Of course, making your own syrups and cordials (*see* page 6) to keep on hand to blend into your favorite cocktails means you can have your favorite mixers at the ready whenever thirsts need sweet slaking.

ISLAND GIN & JUICE

SERVES 1   This trendy cocktail gets an exotic note from orgeat, the orange- and rose-scented almond syrup that is a staple sweetener of tiki drinks. This tropical G & J is delicious poured over coconut water "rocks" instead of regular ice.

2 ounces gin, such as Dorothy Parker

2 ounces freshly squeezed grapefruit juice

1 ounce freshly squeezed lime juice

½ ounce orgeat or Cheater's Orgeat (*see* page 8)

½ Grenadine (*see* page 7)

Lime wedge

Grapefruit peel twist

Combine the gin, grapefruit juice, lime juice, orgeat, and grenadine in a cocktail shaker; dry shake for 30 seconds. Pour over ice in a rocks glass. Garnish with a lime wedge and grapefruit peel twist.

TIP: To make this drink with coconut "rocks," freeze coconut water in an ice-cube tray. Enjoy the subtle flavors that bloom in the glass as the ice melts.

BOURBON-MAPLE SWEET TEA THYME

SERVES 1 Muddling the thyme with the lemon wedges and maple syrup is key to releasing the herb's distinctive flavor. Maple and bourbon are delicious dance partners in this spirited spin on a refreshing sweet tea–meets-lemonade drink that Arnold Palmer made famous.

1 lemon

3 thyme sprigs

1½ ounces maple syrup

2 ounces bourbon

6 ounces chilled brewed black tea

Lemon wedge

Fresh thyme sprig

Cut the lemon in half and cut one half into wedges. Combine the lemon wedges, 2 thyme sprigs, and maple syrup in the bottom of a shaker. Muddle well to release the lemon juices and bruise the thyme. Add the bourbon, tea, and juice from the remaining lemon half and stir well. Pour into an ice-filled pint glass or mason jar. Garnish with a lemon wedge and thyme sprig.

PANTRY GEM

Maple syrup is a star flavoring in drinks, baked goods, and savory dishes. There is a relatively new grading system based on a syrup's flavor and color: golden, amber, dark, and very dark. What used to be the prized "Grade B maple syrup" is now called "Grade A Dark Robust" and it is notable for its dark hue and rich maple flavor that shines in cocktails and cooking.

JAM JAR COCKTAILS

Jam, jelly, and preserves are all tasty stand-ins for muddled fresh fruit, fruit syrups, and even some liqueurs—thin some blackcurrant jam for crème de cassis and cherry preserves for kirsch in a pinch when you want the fruit's flavor note without the big liqueur investment. When just a scrape or two is left in a jelly jar, it's easy to shake up one of these cocktails right inside. Wash and save the jars to use as drinking glasses for future cocktails. Just pour the cocktail from a cocktail shaker into the jar and enjoy, secure the lid, and store the premade drinks in your fridge or freezer until cocktail hour. Give the jars a shake when you're ready to enjoy, add ice if you want, and sip away. If drinking from a jar is too lowbrow for you, simply pour the pre-chilled drinks into a proper coupe, rocks, or highball glass and toast your refrigerator for its resourcefulness.

APPLE BUTTER MANHATTAN
MARMALADE CAIPIRINHA
BLACKBERRY SIDECAR
APRICOT COLLINS

APPLE BUTTER MANHATTAN

SERVES 1   This tastes like autumn in a glass after a day of apple picking. The apple butter adds both a warm spice and a pleasing body to the drink, plus it plays nicely with the whiskey. You could use thyme in place of the rosemary or try tarragon, which also complements apple butter beautifully.

2 ounces rye or bourbon

½ ounce sweet vermouth

2 dashes Angostura bitters

2 teaspoons apple butter

¼ teaspoon minced fresh
   rosemary

Apple wedge

Fresh rosemary sprig

Combine the rye or bourbon, vermouth, bitters, apple butter, and rosemary in a shaker with ice. Shake vigorously and strain into an ice-filled rocks glass. Garnish with an apple wedge and rosemary sprig.

MARMALADE CAIPIRINHA

SERVES 1   The interplay of fruit and spice that shine through in orange marmalade makes it a great choice for a jammy cocktail, like this spin on Brazil's signature Caipirinha. You start by muddling sugar and lime (and in this case a bit of marmalade) together before adding the liquor—traditionally cachaça, though white rum may be used. Like Champagne is to France, cachaça is unique to Brazil and is distilled from fermented sugar cane juice, while rum can be made in many places and is most often made from molasses, a by-product of sugar production.

½ lime, cut into 4 wedges

2 teaspoons demerara sugar

2 teaspoons orange
   marmalade

2 ounces cachaça

Lime wheel

Orange peel twist

Muddle the lime wedges, sugar, and marmalade in the bottom of a rocks glass or half-pint canning jar to release the citrus juices, dissolve the sugar, and incorporate the marmalade. Add the cachaça and ice and stir well. Garnish with a lime wheel and orange peel twist.

PANTRY GEM
I don't have a sweet tooth, but for making cocktails, having an array of sugar types on hand is helpful. Superfine sugar dissolves quickly when shaking a simple syrup. Regular granulated sugar is my go-to. Brown sugars can add notes of molasses to a drink. Other sugars like sanding sugar and demerara sugar are great for rimming glasses or when you need something coarse to help with the work of muddling ingredients.

BLACKBERRY SIDECAR

SERVES 1   Make this sour cocktail in the style of a "brandy crusta" by dampening the rim of a stemmed glass with lemon juice or a bit of the blackberry jam and dipping it in demerara or light brown sugar and straining the drink to serve straight up without ice.

1 tablespoon blackberry jam

1½ ounces cognac or brandy

½ ounce orange liqueur, such as Grand Marnier

½ ounce freshly squeezed lemon juice

Fresh blackberries

Orange peel twist

Combine the jam and brandy in a shaker and stir well with a barspoon to blend. Add the liqueur, lemon juice and ice, and shake vigorously. Strain into a rocks glass or ½ pint canning jar. Garnish with a cocktail pick threaded with blackberries and an orange peel twist.

SNEAKY CHEAT
You're probably more apt to have cognac or brandy on hand than prune juice, but the dried plum nectar is a decent, albeit tamer, stand-in for the distilled grape liquor if you need one.

APRICOT COLLINS

SERVES 1   This Collins variation is a nice ode to the apricot that incorporates both the fruit and a bit of amaretto, a bittersweet, nutty liqueur that is made from the kernels inside apricot pits and sometimes almonds. It is said that the same family that invented the amaretto cookie created the liqueur in Saronno, Italy, in the late 1800s. If you don't have amaretto, substitute orgeat here.

2 ounces vodka

2 tablespoons apricot jam

1 ounce freshly squeezed lemon juice

½ ounce amaretto or Cheater's Orgeat (*see* page 8)

Club soda

Fresh mint sprig

Combine the vodka, apricot jam, lemon juice, and amaretto in a shaker with ice. Shake vigorously. Strain into a highball glass. Top with club soda and stir. Garnish with a mint sprig.

TIP: For a more minty flavor, add a mint sprig to the shaker and muddle with ice before shaking and straining into the glass.

THREE STRIPES YOU'RE OUT

SERVES 1   This layered shot, or pousse-café, combines the bashed and beloved B-52 with the maligned and revered chocolate martini. It's an opportunity to impress your guests with your bartending skills, plus it's a fun nightcap served in a tall shot glass. Build the layers on a foundation of chocolate syrup. The trick is to layer the drink by the density of the liquids. Top the heavy syrup with the liqueur and then add the heavy cream last. Pour each layer after the first very slowly over the back of a spoon so as not to displace the liquid in the layer beneath. Sip the drink layer by layer or stir to mix before you indulge. For a candy corn effect, use orange Curaçao as the middle layer and build it in a small, triangular martini or Nick and Nora glass.

½ to 1 ounce cold chocolate syrup, such as Hershey's

1 ounce liqueur of choice

1 to 1½ ounces heavy cream

Orange peel twist

Pour the chocolate syrup in the bottom of the glass. Use ½ ounce if using a triangular glass and use 1 ounce if using a straight-sided glass for even layers.

Pour 1 ounce of the liqueur very slowly over the back of a spoon so that it floats on top of the syrup.

Pour the heavy cream over the back of the spoon very slowly so that it floats above the liqueur without disturbing the layers. Use 1½ ounces if using a triangular glass or use 1 ounce if using a straight-sided glass for even layers.

NOTE: To make other layered drinks, search for "alcohol density charts" online to know which liquid to pour first, middle, and last.

POUSSE-CAFÉ SHOTS
WITH DISTINCT LAYERS

Chocolate syrup + crème de menthe (mint; clear or green) + heavy cream

Chocolate syrup + kirsch (cherry; clear) + heavy cream

Chocolate syrup + sloe gin (plum; red) + heavy cream

Chocolate syrup + Chambord (raspberry; purple) + heavy cream

Chocolate syrup + cinnamon schnapps (clear) + heavy cream

Chocolate syrup + crème de cassis (black currant; dark red) + heavy cream

Chocolate syrup + Goldschläger (cinnamon; clear with gold flecks) + heavy cream

Chocolate syrup + Sweet Revenge (strawberry; pink) + heavy cream

Chocolate syrup + Apry (apricot; orange) + heavy cream

Chocolate syrup + crème de banane (banana; yellow) + heavy cream

Pickle & Brine Cocktails

The global pickle market is nothing to pucker at. It's a dozen-plus-billion-dollar industry that includes countless jars of pickled vegetables and fruits, pickle potato chips, pickle popcorn, pickle hot sauce, pickle juice soda pop and dill pickle nuts, to name just a few puckering products. Pregnant women are notorious for craving them, and everyday athletes now turn to pickle sports drinks to replenish electrolytes. Perhaps the pickle and brine made their way into cocktails for a similar reason . . . to counteract the dehydrating qualities of alcohol with the potassium-replenishing properties of those gems of the pickle jar. Whether it's a skewer of caperberries and pickled okra in your Bloody Mary, olive brine in your martini, or a gulp of pickle juice to chase that shot of Irish whiskey, there is more than a peck of ways to enjoy pickle tipples.

DIRTY DRY MARTINI

SERVES 1   Some like it salty, so increase the amount of olive brine here to dirty it up to your taste. What makes this a "dry martini" is the touch of dry vermouth instead of sweet. Make it a "sweet martini" by using red vermouth, a "perfect martini" with equal portions of sweet and dry vermouth, or a "wet martini" by upping the ratio of whatever vermouth you use in the mix.

3 ounces London Dry Gin or vodka

½ to 1 teaspoon olive brine

½ ounce dry vermouth

3 pitted olives

Chill a martini glass in the freezer for at least 15 minutes.

Combine the gin or vodka and olive brine in a shaker half-filled with ice. Shake vigorously.

Add the vermouth to the chilled glass and swirl to coat the interior. Toss out the excess. Strain the martini into the prepared glass. Garnish with the olives threaded on a cocktail pick.

FILTHY MARTINI

Substitute caperberry brine for olive brine and garnish with a caperberry or two.

PICKLE BACK

SERVES 1 The bestselling Irish whiskey in the world is Jameson, which ironically was founded by a Scotsman. The popular pickle juice chaser for a shot of whiskey originated in the American South with a shot of bourbon, yet somehow became the popular signature offering at Brooklyn's Bushwick Country Club. The brine does indeed temper the burn and bite of the alcohol.

1½ ounces Irish whiskey, such as Jameson
1½ ounces pickle brine
Dill pickle spear

Pour the Irish whiskey in a shot glass. Pour the pickle brine in a separate shot glass with the pickle spear.

Drink the whiskey and chase it with the pickle brine. Enjoy the pickle spear.

PANTRY GEM
Don't toss the juice from the pickle, olive, caper, kimchi, or kraut jar. Enlist all of these tart and salty liquids into cocktail service or your cooking. Brine chicken in any of these before dredging and frying, marinate your holiday bird in a pickle juice bath before roasting, or stir a bit of the juice into coleslaw, tartar sauce, or a vinaigrette for mouthwatering interest.

PICKLE BARREL MARTINIS

Few drinks feel more sophisticated than a martini. Whether it's the distinctive glass in which it is served or the drink's place in pop culture, it somehow feels cultivated and worldly to order, hold, and sip one. With the exception of a few small additions, a modern martini is basically an ample serving of chilled straight booze. What makes it a cocktail instead of a shot is the addition of vermouth, an aromatized fortified wine that can be dry or sweet and sometimes a dash or two of olive brine, which turns the liquid cloudy, making it a dirty martini. Olive brine might be the usual dirty player, but as these recipes prove, any brine will do.

DIRTY DRY MARTINI
KIMCHI VESPER
SWEET PICKLE GIMLET

KIMCHI VESPER

SERVES 1   Ian Fleming, creator of James Bond, also created the Vesper cocktail, named for the double-agent Vesper Lynd, which appeared in his 1953 novel *Casino Royale*. A bartending rule is to stir drinks composed solely of spirits and save the shaking for drinks that include mixers. I defer to James Bond's wishes—shaken not stirred—in this briny rendition. If you make this cocktail with vodka rather than soju it will be a more potent drink.

3 ounces gin

1 ounce soju (see note) or vodka

½ ounce mirin or red vermouth

1 tablespoon kimchi brine

1 piece kimchi threaded onto a cocktail pick (optional)

Chill a cocktail glass in the freezer for at least 15 minutes.

Combine the gin, soju or vodka, mirin, and kimchi brine in a shaker half-filled with ice. Shake vigorously. Strain into the chilled martini glass. Garnish with kimchi, if desired.

NOTE: Soju is a low-ABV Korean spirit that is similar to vodka and is distilled from rice or sweet potatoes. The Japanese make a similar spirit called shochu. Both are becoming more common in the United States in cocktails and sipped alone. Mirin is a sweet Japanese fermented rice wine that is lower in alcohol than sake. It is often used in cooking and is readily available on the global aisle of most supermarkets.

SWEET PICKLE GIMLET

SERVES 1 Some say that the classic gin gimlet should always be made with Rose's Sweetened Lime Juice. This tart-sweet viscose liquid has slightly bitter afternotes thanks to ingredients like high-fructose corn syrup that you might normally snub, but some sort of alchemy occurs when it melds with the resinous notes of gin. I forgo it here because fresh lime juice mixed with sweet pickle brine works fine in my opinion and is something you are likely to have on hand.

1½ ounces **London Dry Gin**

½ ounce **sweet pickle brine, such as Wickles Original**

½ ounce **freshly squeezed lime juice**

Thin lime wheel

Combine the gin, pickle juice, and lime juice in a shaker with ice. Stir with a barspoon. Strain into a chilled coupe glass. Float a lime wheel on the surface of the drink

PANTRY GEM

A ninety-year-old secret Alabama family recipe became a national sensation when Wickles Pickles Original hit the market in 1998. The fat-cut pickle chips are packed in a sweet-and-savory brine that created a cult following. When the jar of pickles is empty, save the pickle juice for mixing or cooking. Add it to a Bloody Mary or stir it into egg or chicken salad. It is also a worthy chaser for a shot of Jameson whiskey in a Pickle Back (*see page 36*).

SALTY PEPERONCINI PERRO

SERVES 1 Spicy, salty, zesty peperoncini brine boosts the saline spark of this variation on the Salty Dog cocktail made with blanco tequila instead of vodka. For the best sweet-tart flavor, choose a Texas red grapefruit like Ruby Red or a pomelo, a cross between a grapefruit and orange with pink flesh and a sweet tang.

2 teaspoons coarse kosher salt

2 teaspoons grapefruit zest

1 grapefruit wedge

2 ounces blanco tequila

4 ounces freshly squeezed grapefruit juice

2 teaspoons peperoncini brine

Grapefruit twist

If desired, make the Grapefruit Rim Salt. Combine the salt and grapefruit zest on a saucer. Rub the lip of an old-fashioned glass with the grapefruit wedge. Invert the glass on the saucer and twist to coat the rim. This will rim 2 to 3 drinks.

Fill the glass with ice. Add the tequila, grapefruit juice, and peperoncini brine to the glass. Stir well. Garnish with a grapefruit twist.

PANTRY GEM
I used the brine from Jeff's Garden Greek Peperoncini for this cocktail. The tangy brine is delicious tossed with warm cubed potatoes, olive oil, Greek yogurt, lemon zest, chopped parsley, green onions, and lots of black pepper for an uncommonly delicious picnic potato salad. Add lots of the chopped peperoncini, too, of course.

Egg & Dairy Cocktails

The addition of dairy lends body to cocktails while buffering the alcohol's burn. Fridge staples like eggs blended into cocktails work similar magic, adding a rich and luxurious mouthfeel to drinks. Thanks to their fat content, dairy, eggs, and egg yolks are wonderful carriers of flavor that temper strong boozy notes, while egg whites alone can transform the texture of a drink with airy heft and no added fat. Not all egg and dairy cocktails are mind-numbing milkshakes. The New Orleans Gin Fizz (*see* page 46), that famous frothy forever-shaken favorite, tastes light and refreshing, egg white and cream aside. A full-bodied, whole-egg Spiced Sherry Flip (*see* page 48) is a slow sipper that satisfies in a one-and-done way, making it an ideal nightcap. Dairy punches like the classic Bourbon Milk Punch (*see* page 45) and novel Liquid Lunch (*see* page 49) are rich and luscious without weighing you down, so that perhaps there's room for seconds.

BOURBON MILK PUNCH

SERVES 1   There is milk punch and then there is clarified milk punch. The latter is punch that uses the coagulation that happens when milk and citrus combine as a means to capture and remove impurities from a liquid, rendering it clear, or clarified. This is the former—a citrus-free old-world punch of whiskey or brandy (though sometimes rum or sherry) mixed with milk and sugar that gained renewed popularity in New Orleans in the nineteenth century. Served over ice, it was sometimes called "ponche au lait" in Creole parlance. It may also be served warm.

1 wafer-style cookie, like Nilla, a pecan sandie, or shortbread

2 teaspoons sanding sugar

3 ounces whole milk, plus additional for rimming the glass

1½ ounces bourbon

½ ounce dark rum

1 ounce Simple Syrup (*see page 6*)

2-inch piece vanilla bean, scraped, or ¼ teaspoon vanilla extract

Grated nutmeg

If desired, make the Cookie-Crumb Rim Sugar. Place the cookie in a zip-top sandwich bag and roll over it with a rolling pin to create fine crumbs. Combine with the sanding sugar on a small plate. Dampen the rim of rocks glass with milk. Invert the glass on the plate and twist to coat the rim. This will rim about 2 drinks.

Combine the milk, bourbon, rum, simple syrup, vanilla bean paste, and scraped pod into a shaker with ice. Shake vigorously. Strain into the glass with or without ice and garnish with freshly grated nutmeg.

SNEAKY CHEAT

For an easy, rich milk punch, combine a melted scoop of vanilla ice cream with the bourbon and rum and forego the milk, simple syrup, and vanilla bean altogether.

NEW ORLEANS GIN FIZZ

SERVES 1   Also called the Ramos Gin Fizz, this is a fine drink born of pomp and pre-Prohibition circumstance at Henry C. Ramos's Imperial Cabinet Saloon, where two dozen bartenders would shake each drink for twelve minutes before pouring them for an adoring crowd. It doesn't need to be a bicep-builder; a two-minute shake following a dry shake does the trick nicely.

1½ ounces gin

½ ounce freshly squeezed lime juice

½ ounce freshly squeezed lemon juice

2 ounces heavy cream

2 ounces Rich Simple Syrup (*see* page 6)

1 large egg white

½ teaspoon orange flower water

Club soda

Orange wedge

Chill a Collins glass.

Add the gin, citrus juices, cream, simple syrup, egg white, and orange flower to a shaker without ice. Dry shake for 30 seconds. Add ice to the shaker and shake vigorously for 2 minutes to emulsify the ingredients.

Add 1 ounce club soda to the chilled glass and strain the cocktail into the glass. Top with more soda so that the raft of foam rises just above the rim of the glass. Garnish with an orange wedge.

SPICED SHERRY FLIP

SERVES 1   This sweet cocktail has been around for centuries and gets its rich, full body from the whole egg and syrup used. Flips are traditionally made with robust spirits like bourbon, rye, dark rum or fortified wines, or a mix of two. This sherry shake-up tastes like liquid raisins scented with cardamom. It is an enchanting after-dinner drink. A small dose of lemon juice and pinch of salt really amplify the flavors.

2 ounces sweet sherry, such as Lustau PX or East India Solera

½ ounce freshly squeezed lemon juice

1 ounce Honey Syrup (*see* page 7)

1 large egg, beaten

3 drops cardamom bitters (optional)

Salt

Dash ground cardamom

Grated shelled pistachio

Combine the sherry, lemon juice, honey syrup, egg, and bitters, if using, and a tiny pinch of salt in a shaker without ice. Dry shake. Add ice and vigorously shake 30 seconds to chill. Double strain into a sherry or Nick and Nora glass. Garnish with a pinch of cardamom and a grating of pistachio.

TIP: When you need just a bit of lemon juice, like a tablespoon or less, roll a lemon between your palm and the counter and then puncture it with the point of knife. Squeeze out just the amount of juice you need. A whole lemon will keep longer. Just be sure it's the first in rotation next time you need a lemon.

SNEAKY CHEAT
If you don't have sherry, use the fortified wine you have in your fridge from cooking if it's good. Each can be shaken into a frothy flip—madeira or port from Portugal; marsala from Sicily; vermouth from Italy, France, or Spain; or cognac from France. Start simply with just 3 parts wine, 1 part syrup, and 1 egg, and then experiment with complementary bitters, spices, or juices to accentuate the flavor profile.

LIQUID LUNCH

SERVES 1   This is a PB&J and a glass of ice-cold milk poured into one.
A sweet cordial made from a Concord grape juice reduction melds with dark
rum that has been fat-washed with peanut butter for an adult take on a childhood
favorite. You can opt to fat-wash bourbon or vodka, too. For a fun embellishment,
rub the rim of the glass with a grape half or a bit of grape cordial and invert the
glass into a dish with a thin layer of powdered peanut butter.

1 ounce Concord Grape
   Cordial (*recipe follows*)

2 ounces Peanut Butter–
   Washed Rum (*recipe
   follows*)

3 ounces whole milk

3 purple grapes

1 salt-roasted peanut

Combine the grape cordial, rum, and milk in a shaker with
ice. Shake vigorously. Strain over a large ice cube in a rocks
glass. Garnish with a cocktail pick threaded with purple
grapes. Use a microplane grater to grate the peanut over
the surface of the drink.

CONCORD GRAPE CORDIAL

Heat 1 cup Concord grape juice and 1 cup sugar to a simmer in
a small saucepan over medium-high heat. Reduce heat to low
and cook, stirring occasionally, until the liquid is reduced by
half. Whisk 1 teaspoon fresh lemon juice into the syrup and
transfer it to a clean bottle. **Makes about ¾ cup.**

PEANUT BUTTER–WASHED RUM

Combine 8 ounces dark rum with 1 ounce of the oil from the
top of a jar of organic peanut butter in a freezer-safe container.
Cover, shake vigorously, and set aside in a cool, dark place at
room temperature for 24 to 48 hours. Transfer the container to
the freezer for 8 hours or overnight to allow the oil to separate
and solidify. Remove the layer of oil and strain the rum though
a cheesecloth-lined strainer. **Makes 8 ounces.**

THE SPEAKEASY BOARD

Before we married, my husband John and I spent many nights in San Francisco with friends at a speakeasy on Haight Street called Club Deluxe, where we listened to great music and loved to people-watch. On any given night there was an amazingly diverse crowd—grandparents, hippies, yuppies, and rockabilly 1950s wannabes—who all came together to listen to some of the best jazz ensembles around. It was owned by the late, great crooner Jay Johnson, who had a voice that rivaled Frank Sinatra's, and who I am so lucky to say sang at my wedding reception. I don't even remember if they served food at Club Deluxe, but the drinks were great and the memories priceless. This food board serves up delicacies from the same Dixieland region where jazz was born.

Creamy Remoulade,
PAGE 133

Cajun Chicken Pops,
PAGE 153

West Indies Salad,
PAGE 152

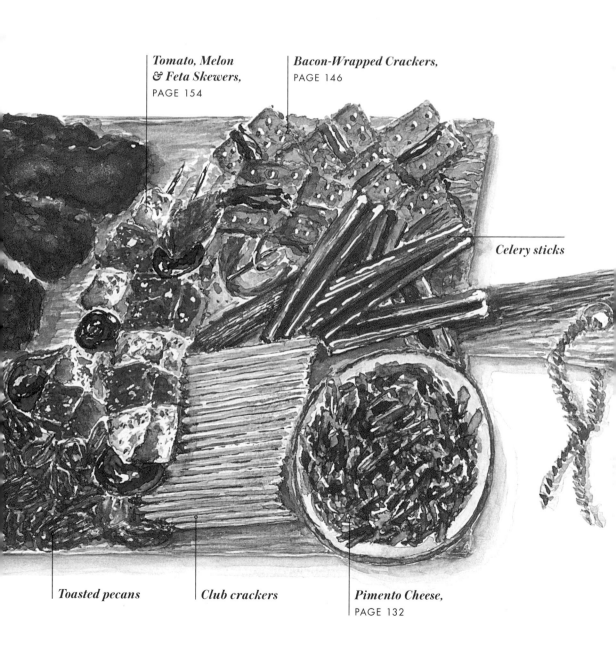

Tomato, Melon & Feta Skewers, PAGE 154

Bacon-Wrapped Crackers, PAGE 146

Celery sticks

Toasted pecans

Club crackers

Pimento Cheese, PAGE 132

THAI-ONE-ON ICED TEA

SERVES 1   This is a sweet and refreshing cocktail that's ideal for enjoying on a hot summer evening. It's also a great way to use that nondairy coffee creamer taking up room in the fridge. If you have access to Mekhong whiskey, this would be the perfect cocktail to use it. It is not really whiskey, but rather a distillation of sugar cane, molasses, rice, and Thai herbs that is closer to rum or cachaça in style.

- **4 ounces freshly brewed Thai tea**
- **1 tablespoon sugar**
- **1 (6-inch) lemongrass stalk, split lengthwise**
- **2 ounces gold rum**
- **2 tablespoons half-and-half, nondairy creamer, or coconut cream**
- **Fresh mint sprig**

Pour the hot tea over the sugar in a highball glass. Smash a lemongrass stalk half with a meat mallet or bank it with a heavy skillet to bruise it, then place it in the glass. Stir the tea with the stalk to help the heat dissipate and infuse the tea with lemongrass flavor. Set aside for 5 minutes.

Pack the glass with ice, add the rum, and stir with the lemongrass stalk to mix and chill. Pour in the half-and-half, nondairy creamer, or coconut cream, and stir. Garnish with a mint sprig.

PANTRY GEM

Pantai imported Thai tea mix is a restaurant favorite with that quintessential taste and vivid orange hue. I prefer Arbor Teas Organic Thai Iced Tea blend, which has no artificial yellow dyes. No matter the brand, use Thai tea to infuse crème anglaise for Thai tea ice cream, steep with water and salt to make a flavorful brine for poultry, or add the crumbled tea to shortbread dough for exotic tea-spiced cookies.

2

GARDEN

There is an old saying that a garden adds years to your life and life to your years. It also adds life to your cooking and cocktails. You don't need acres, or even a backyard, to grow a bounty of herbs and a vegetable or two. A couple of pots on a balcony or windowsill will do. Edible plants can add flavor, color, and pretty embellishment to drinks. They can flavor syrups, infuse spirits, or be blended into the cocktail mix as a starring ingredient. A homegrown pansy or nasturtium blossom is as pretty a garnish on the rim of a glass as a pricey store-bought orchid floating atop a tiki drink. Growing and harvesting is satisfying in so many ways, and somehow drinks taste better when made with something freshly plucked from plant or ground. Seek out varieties of ingredients that you can grow in your area and include some unique ones that you can't find at the grocery store. Enjoy your harvests, compost leftovers, and get scrappy. When you've used up all the celery as the stirrers for a batch of Bloody Marys, don't toss the root base. Simply pop into soil, set it in the sunshine, water it, and watch it grow again. In no time, you'll have homegrown crudités for a food board or the makings for a distinctive cordial or vegetal tipple you can create on the fly.

Herbal Cocktails

I put herbs in everything . . . e v e r y t h i n g! Chives and chervil in scrambled eggs, mint in my water bottle, salad leaf basil on grilled cheese sandwiches, French tarragon in chicken salad, and a different herb or two in the half dozen vinaigrettes I whip up each week. I love herb-y sauces and relishes—chimichurri, salsa verde, pesto, gremolata, and persillade. I make herb salts, infused oils, and aiolis. Every sprig or leaf that I cannot use gets finely minced and spooned into ice cube trays with a bit of water to preserve them for when winter is coming and my garden goes dormant. Sure, I buy staple fresh herbs from the grocery store, but in warm weather, growing them is so easy that it's a no-brainer. I scour seed catalogs to order herbs like shiso, burnet, lovage, chamomile, borage, rapunzel, angelica, rarer varieties of mint, basil, sage, and other flavor-packed herbs that I never could find at my supermarket, but that add incomparable interest to dishes and drinks. Use Thai basil in place of mint in a mojito. Try lemongrass and kaffir lime leaf in a Far East riff on the Moscow Mule (*see* page 60), or make any summertime slush even more refreshing by tossing a handful of mint into the blender.

BASIL-MINT G & T

SERVES 1   This G & T gets its sweetness from a complex lime-and-herb cordial that stands in for the usual lime juice alone. Change up the herbs to suit your tastes. Try pineapple mint, shiso leaf, chervil, lemongrass, and so on. I always turn to light or unsweetened varieties of tonic water because regular tonic packs as much sugar as soda pop.

1 fresh Thai basil sprig

1 fresh mint sprig

3 ounces gin

¾ ounce Peppery Lime-Herb Cordial (*recipe follows*)

4 ounces tonic water, such as Navy Hill soda + tonic

1 lime wedge

Clap the basil and mint sprigs between your palms to bruise slightly and release their aromatic oils. Drop them into a highball glass. Add the gin and cordial. Fill the glass with ice and top off with the tonic. Stir. Garnish with a lime wedge.

PEPPERY LIME-HERB CORDIAL

Remove the strips of zest from 6 to 8 limes with a vegetable peeler. Set aside. Juice the limes to yield 1 cup. Combine the fresh lime juice and ½ cup superfine sugar in a quart-size lidded container. Shake vigorously until the sugar is dissolved. Add the reserved lime peels, 1 tablespoon minced fresh mint, and 6 crushed black peppercorns to the syrup. Cover and refrigerate for 8 to 12 hours. Strain and add ½ ounce overproof vodka. Store in the refrigerator up to 2 weeks. **Makes about 1 cup.**

CHIANG MAI MULE

SERVES 1 Lemongrass is easy to grow and a pretty back-of-the-border garden plant. Or use it as the "thriller" component in a pot of mixed herbs. Every pot should have a thriller, a filler, and a spiller. I grow tall lemongrass in the back of a large narrow pot, bushy Thai basil in the middle, and trailing spearmint in front. All three of these herbs would work well here, but the kaffir lime leaf from an Asian variety of fruitless lime adds a truly distinctive flavor to this drink. It's a small container tree worth growing. Just bring it inside before the first frost.

1 lime slice

1 slice fresh ginger root

1 fresh or frozen kaffir lime leaf, torn

1 (3-inch) piece lemongrass stalk

2 ounces vodka

½ ounce freshly squeezed lime juice

6 ounces ginger ale, such as Buffalo Rock

Kaffir lime leaf

Lime wheel

Lemongrass stalk (optional)

Combine the lime, ginger, kaffir lime leaf, and lemongrass in a cocktail shaker. Muddle to bruise and release their flavor. Add ice and the vodka and lime juice to the shaker and shake vigorously. Strain into a copper mug. Top with the ginger ale. Garnish with a kaffir lime leaf, lime wheel, and lemongrass stalk for stirring, if desired.

TIP: For a cheap, chemical-free way to keep your copper mugs and cookware tarnish-free and gleaming, coat them in ketchup or yogurt from your fridge and then walk away for half an hour while they work their magic. Simply rinse and buff dry to shiny perfection.

HERB GARDEN SLUSHIES

Some scream for ice cream, but snow cones, convenience-store Icees, sorbet, and boardwalk shaved ices all scream summertime in the most refreshing way, too. It's like a vacation in a glass, so why not spike it with something spirited and something fresh from the garden? Bubbly prosecco and tart limoncello shine brighter with a bunch of basil in the mix. Eye-opening mint updates the age-old Silver Monk (*see* page 65) in a cooling adult slush. If you don't know shiso, she'll become your new favorite herb to grow after one sip of a Shiso Lovely Mango Fuzzy (*see* page 66) and lavender lends a floral feminine note to Hemingway's usual, and it's so tasty it may just become yours.

BASIL-CELLO FROSECCO
MINTY SILVER MONK SLUSHIES
SHISO LOVELY MANGO FUZZIES
LAVENDER DAIQUIRIS

BASIL-CELLO FROSECCO

SERVES 8 This herb-and-citrus mash-up gets a distinctive note from a touch of amaretto, the popular almond-flavored liqueur that, surprisingly, is made from apricot pits. If you don't have amaretto, add a teaspoon of almond syrup or splash of almond extract to the blender and top off the drink with a bit more prosecco.

8 ounces limoncello

4 ounces Citrus Oleo Saccharum (see page 7)

4 ounces amaretto

12 fresh basil leaves

Prosecco

8 fresh basil sprigs

Blend the limoncello, oleo saccharum, amaretto, and basil leaves in a blender. Transfer to a 9 x 13-inch baking dish. Slowly pour in the prosecco, stirring to combine. Freeze for 2½ hours and then remove, breaking up the ice with a fork. Return to the freezer and repeat the process every half hour until it is the desired slush consistency. Spoon into champagne flutes and garnish each with a basil sprig.

TIP: When you have a bit of prosecco or champagne left in the bottle (it does happen), leave it uncorked in the fridge overnight so the bubbly goes flat. Make ice cubes with it to float in your brunch mimosa, use it in place of champagne vinegar in a vinaigrette, or as you would white wine in recipes.

MINTY SILVER MONK SLUSHIES

SERVES 4 The Silver Monk cocktail gets its name from the Carthusian monks who have been making liqueur in the Chartreuse Mountains of France near Grenoble since the 1700s. There are so many liqueurs worth adding to your liquor cabinet, and I think Chartreuse is one. It is made from 130 botanicals, so it's very complex. If you don't have it, know that it brings very sweet and complex herbal notes to a drink. Nothing replicates it, but you could create a mixed herb simple syrup using tarragon, fennel, and chervil, adding the flavors of licorice, cinnamon, and citrus to infuse a drink with similar qualities. For a less expensive Chartreuse swap, use Dolin Génépy des Alpes liqueur here instead.

12 fresh mint leaves

10 peeled cucumber slices

1 cup Simple Syrup
(*see* page 6)

½ teaspoon kosher salt

6 ounces blanco tequila

2 ounces yellow Chartreuse

2 ounces fresh lime juice

4 cucumber spears

4 fresh mint sprigs

Combine 3 cups ice with mint, cucumber slices, syrup, salt, tequila, Chartreuse, and lime juice in a blender, cover with the lid, and process until smooth. Pour into coupe glasses and garnish each with a cucumber spear and mint sprig.

SHISO LOVELY MANGO FUZZIES

SERVES 6 Tart and refreshing, frozen mango stands in for peaches to give this fuzzy lots of fuzzless flavor. If you are unfamiliar with shiso, also called perilla and beefsteak plant, it is a green or purple-leafed citrusy herb with hints of spice that is easy to grow and adds so much flavor to fish, rice, soups, and vinaigrettes. You might have seen the sawtooth-edged leaves on a sushi or sashimi platter. Don't let them go to waste. Like cilantro, the flavor of shiso can be polarizing, so if you find you're not a fan, substitute mint, basil, or even tarragon here.

1 (12-ounce) can limeade concentrate

8 ounces vodka

1 (10½-ounce) can coconut water, such as Taste Nirvana

1 (16-ounce) bag frozen mango chunks

6 fresh green shiso leaves

6 lime wedges

Combine the limeade concentrate, vodka, coconut water, mango chunks, and shiso leaves in a blender. Cover with the lid and blend until smooth. Remove the lid and add 3 cups ice. Cover again and blend until smooth. Pour into hurricane glasses and serve each with a lime wedge.

PANTRY GEM
Coconut water is trendy and tasty—sometimes. There are a lot of bad ones out there that taste like coconut extract or suntan lotion–infused water. I've taste-tested too many like that, so I find myself reaching for the Taste Nirvana brand time and time again. It is 100% pure coconut water harvested from prized Nam Hom coconuts grown in the fertile Nakorn Pathom region of Thailand, with no additives or preservatives.

LAVENDER DAIQUIRIS

SERVES 4 TO 6 Lavender fields are something to behold. Growing it out West, I felt like I had a purple thumb. In the South, it has flopped for me every time. After all, lavender loves heat, just not a blanket of humidity. When I saw a grower selling potted lavender at a local farmers' market, I thought surely he was setting buyers up for failure. He explained it was "phenomenal lavender" and I retorted, "Yeah, is that the best you can come up with?" Then he explained it is an actual variety called "phenomenal" that was bred for the South's chewable summer air. Two summers later, and much to my amazement, it has survived. I put bundles of cut flower stems in a vase without water and let them dry on my kitchen windowsill. I pull off the tiny dried blossoms and put them in a spice jar in the cupboard to use in cooking. You can do this with whatever culinary variety you have or grow.

8 ounces white rum

4 ounces fresh lemon juice

4 ounces Lavender Simple Syrup (*recipe follows*)

½ ounce crème de violette, such as Rothman & Winter (optional)

4 to 6 lavender blossoms

Combine the rum, lemon juice, syrup, crème de violette, if using, and about 6 cups ice in a blender. Cover with the lid and blend until smooth. Divide among 4 to 6 coupe glasses and garnish each with a lavender blossom.

LAVENDER SIMPLE SYRUP

Combine 1 cup water, 1 cup sugar, and 3 tablespoons dried or ½ cup fresh lavender blossoms (strip the petals from the stems, if using fresh, to measure) in a small saucepan over low heat, whisking until the sugar is fully dissolved. Remove from the heat, cool completely, and strain. Transfer the syrup to a clean bottle and refrigerate for up to 2 weeks. **Makes about 1¾ cups.**

SNEAKY CHEAT

If you don't have crème de violette, a handful of fresh or frozen blueberries (about ¼ cup) added to the blender will boost the purplish hue of this drink without adding a dominant berry flavor.

SAGE VICE

SERVES 1   Think of this cocktail as a Rob Roy—a Manhattan made with scotch—but with sage-infused simple syrup in place of the usual sweet vermouth, and a woodsy amaro with bitter wisps of pine and smoke instead of dashes of Angostura. If you haven't developed a taste for scotch, try this cocktail with Dutch genever (or its can-be-made-anywhere cousin confusingly called Holland gin), a distilled malted spirit made from grain and botanicals that is like a hybrid cross of gin and whiskey.

1½ ounces blended scotch or genever

¾ ounce Amaro Pasubio or Cynar

½ ounce Sage Simple Syrup (*recipe follows*)

Orange peel twist

Fresh sage leaf

Combine the scotch, Amaro Pasubio or Cynar, and syrup in a shaker with ice. Stir well to chill. Strain into a rocks glass with a large cube of ice. Garnish with an orange twist expressed over the drink. Clap a sage leaf between your palms and float the leaf on top.

SAGE SIMPLE SYRUP

Combine ½ cup water and ½ cup sugar in a small saucepan over low heat, whisking until the sugar is fully dissolved. Remove from the heat and add ¼ cup loosely packed fresh sage leaves. Cool completely and then strain. Transfer the syrup to a clean bottle and refrigerate for up to 2 weeks. **Makes about ¾ cup.**

THE WINE BAR BOARD

I adore kicking off an evening with a cocktail, but prefer to follow it with a glass of wine. Long before FOMO was an acronym, I felt it. I longed to become a sommelier, but that test! My love affair with wine bloomed while working at a vineyard in Bordeaux in my early twenties and strengthened with the blind wine tastings that closed out each week of culinary school in San Francisco. Winemakers from Napa, Sonoma, Mendocino, Paso Robles, and points beyond educated us while we sipped, savored, and learned to identify the flavors and aromas of each wine. The first week we stuck to the usual words—grassy, earthy, mineral-y—but by graduation we'd honed our palates and confidence as we tossed out descriptors like petrol, tin, juniper, hay, and leather. Like wine tasting, exploring the magic that happens when food is paired with wine is an exercise that never gets old, plus there's no test required.

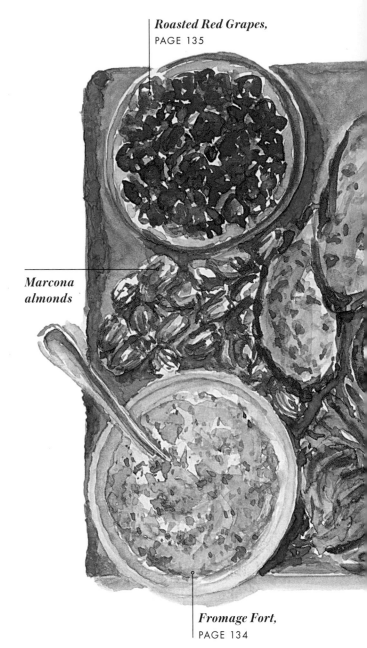

Roasted Red Grapes,
PAGE 135

Marcona almonds

Fromage Fort,
PAGE 134

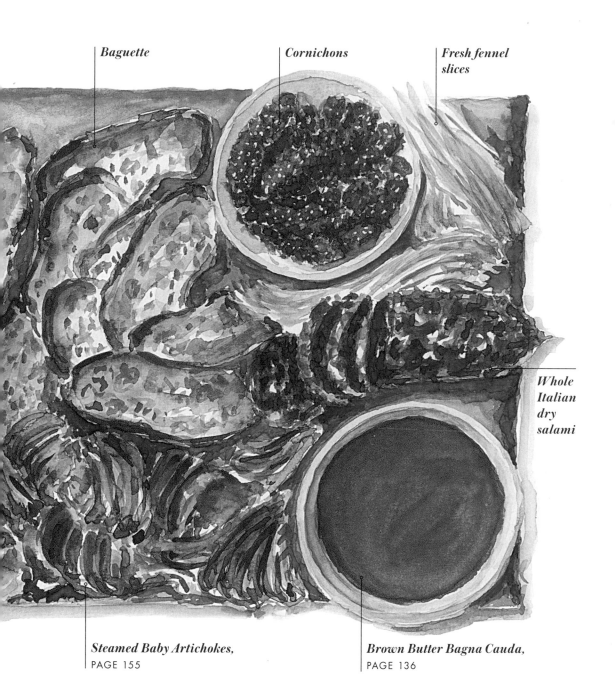

Baguette

Cornichons

Fresh fennel slices

Whole Italian dry salami

Steamed Baby Artichokes,
PAGE 155

Brown Butter Bagna Cauda,
PAGE 136

Vegetable Cocktails

Botanically speaking, several of the "vegetables" highlighted in the handful of cocktails that follow are classified as fruits—avocados, tomatoes, and cucumbers—but for culinary purposes they are most often lumped in the vegetable category, and that's how I have categorized them here. To confuse things further, sometimes a drink is a fusion of vegetable, fruit, and herbs, making it a cocktail candidate for multiple sections of this book, but it's the vegetable component that makes it noteworthy. So often we think that a fruit or vegetable must be muddled or blended into a drink, but there are more subtle ways to infuse a cocktail with vegetal flavor. Take the Glazed-Carrot Old Fashioned (*see* page 73), which fuses a cooked carrot side dish and bourbon and lets it steep for a week before straining and mixing the flavor-infused bourbon into the cocktail. Like the Tomato Water Martini created from the clear liquid essence strained from chopped tomatoes, these drinks are less in-your-face and more nuanced, but oh-so delicious.

GLAZED-CARROT OLD FASHIONED

SERVES 1   The inherent earthy sweetness of carrots pairs well with bourbon and adds an interesting complexity to a classic Old Fashioned. Try this treatment with other roots and spirits—beets, parsnips, rutabagas, and sweet potatoes all add interesting flavor notes to spirited infusions. Know that this requires one full week to prep, but it is worth it. Remember an Old Fashioned is potent. It's a drink to sip slowly and savor . . . unless you want to get your swerve on, of course.

GLAZED-CARROT BOURBON

1 pound baby carrots

½ teaspoon salt

2 tablespoons butter

2 tablespoons brown sugar

Finely grated zest of 1 orange

1 tablespoon freshly squeezed orange juice

1 (375-ml) bottle bourbon

1 raw brown sugar cube

Angostura bitters

2 ounces Glazed-Carrot Bourbon

Baby carrot with leafy top

Orange wheel

Make the Glazed-Carrot Bourbon by bringing a small saucepan of water to a boil. Add the carrots and salt and cook for 5 to 8 minutes or until crisp-tender. Drain and return to the saucepan with the butter, brown sugar, orange zest, and orange juice. Cook over medium-low heat until the sugar has dissolved and the liquid is syrupy and coats the carrots, 3 to 5 minutes. Remove the pan from the heat and let the carrots cool completely.

Transfer the carrots and the glaze to a quart-size jar or nonreactive container and pour the bourbon over the carrots (save the bottle). Cover the jar or container and set it aside at room temperature for 1 week. Strain the bourbon through a cheesecloth- or coffee filter–lined funnel back into the bourbon bottle and label accordingly. **Makes about 12 ounces (1½ cups)**.

Prepare the cocktail by placing the sugar cube in the bottom of a rocks glass. Soak it with a few dashes of bitters. Add a splash of water and muddle the cube until dissolved. Fill the glass with ice and pour the bourbon over. Stir with a barspoon to mix and chill. Garnish with a baby carrot and an orange wheel.

PANTRY GEM

In addition to being a terrific substitute for cheesecloth for straining particles out of liquids, coffee filters are a great tool for cleaning glasses and windows for a streak- and lint-free shine.

TOMATO WATER MARTINI

SERVES 1 Use tomato water to make a "bloodless" Bloody Mary, enjoy it mixed with seltzer and a basil leaf for a refreshing and hydrating mocktail, or create clear tomato aspic to surprise and delight. When tomatoes are in season, I make a big batch of tomato water and freeze it in sandwich bags that I stack flat in my freezer to pull out as needed. Don't think it's a waste of summer tomatoes . . . you still can use all that tomato pulp after the water has been extracted. It is delicious made into salsa; mixed with garlic, basil, and red chili flakes for bruschetta topping; folded into an omelet; tossed with hot cooked pasta . . . you get the picture.

½ ounce dry vermouth

3 ounces vodka or gin

3 ounces Tomato Water (*recipe follows*)

Fresh basil leaf

3 to 4 grape tomatoes or cocktail onions

Add the vermouth to a chilled martini glass and swirl it around to coat the glass.

Combine the vodka or gin and Tomato Water in a shaker with ice. Shake vigorously to chill. Strain into the glass.

Clap the basil leaf between your palms and float it on the surface of the cocktail. Serve with a cocktail skewer of grape tomatoes or cocktail onions.

TOMATO WATER

Core and cut 3 beefsteak tomatoes into chunks. Pulse in a food processor with ½ teaspoon salt until you have a chunky coarse puree. Transfer the tomato pulp to a small mesh strainer lined with a few layers of cheesecloth or a coffee filter set over a bowl. Set aside in the refrigerator at least 8 hours or overnight to allow the juice to separate from the pulp. Do not press on the pulp. You want the tomato water to remain clear. **Makes about 1 cup.**

SWEET CORN FIELDWATER

SERVES 1 This spin on the beloved Texas Ranchwater incorporates muddled sweet corn. The starch in the milky corn juices gives the drink a silky quality and its cloudiness, but also the telltale summery flavor of ripe sweet corn. To cook the corn, bring a pot of water to a rolling boil, add a handful of sea salt, and drop in the corn. Turn off the heat and let the corn sit in the hot water for 10 minutes. It will be kernel perfection!

¼ cup cooked corn kernels from fresh sweet corn

½ ounce agave syrup

1 ounce freshly squeezed lime juice

3 fresh jalapeño slices

2 grapefruit peel strips

2 ounces blanco tequila

Topo Chico sparkling water

1 piece cooked corn on the cob

Muddle the corn, agave syrup, lime juice, jalapeño slices, and 1 grapefruit peel strip in the bottom of a cocktail shaker. Add ice and the tequila. Shake vigorously and strain into a rocks glass with ice and the remaining grapefruit strip. Top with sparkling water. Garnish with a piece of cooked corn on the cob for nibbling while you sip.

SNAP PEA 75

SERVES 1   This is like springtime in a glass and one of my favorite cocktails in this book. It is fresh, sweet, and grassy in a good way. Once you infuse simple syrup with a vegetable this way, a whole new world of flavors opens up to you, and you just may find yourself making syrups with whatever just-harvested vegetable you've procured from your garden, farmers' market, or roadside stand.

1½ ounces London Dry Gin

½ ounce freshly squeezed lemon juice

½ ounce Snap Pea Simple Syrup (*recipe follows*)

2 ounces dry champagne or prosecco

Snap pea

Lemon peel twist

Combine the gin, lemon juice, and syrup in a shaker with ice. Shake vigorously to chill. Strain into a champagne flute. Top with the champagne or prosecco. Garnish with the snap pea and lemon peel twist.

SNAP PEA SIMPLE SYRUP

Blend ¼ pound snap peas (about 1 cup) in a high-speed blender with 8 ounces of water until thoroughly blended. Strain into a glass measuring cup and measure the liquid. Discard the solids. Add an equal measure of superfine sugar. Heat over low heat, stirring until the sugar is dissolved. Remove from the heat to cool. Transfer the syrup to a bottle or jar and refrigerate for up to 3 days. **Makes about 12 ounces (about 1½ cups).**

TIP: Labeling bottles and jars of syrups, cordials, and infusions is key. You don't want to accidentally add Basil Oil (*see* page 154) to this cocktail instead of the Snap Pea Simple Syrup. I save all those wide rubber bands from bundles of supermarket produce and then secure them like belts around jars or bottles. I use a marker to write the name of what's inside on the band so I know what I have on hand.

RHUBARB MOJITO

SERVES 1   Build this drink in a cocktail shaker if you wish to strain out all the rhubarb pieces. I happen to like the interest of the bits of rhubarb and the mint in the glass. If rhubarb is in season and you are using fresh, reserve a stalk for a pretty stir.

2 lemon slices

¼ cup thawed frozen or fresh rhubarb pieces

1 ounce Rhubarb Syrup (*recipe follows*)

6 fresh mint leaves

2 ounces white rum

Club soda

Skinny rhubarb stalk (optional)

Fresh mint sprig

Lemon peel twist

Muddle the lemon slices, rhubarb pieces, syrup, and mint leaves in the bottom of a highball glass. Add the rum and ice. Top off with club soda and stir to mix and chill. Garnish with a rhubarb stalk, if desired, mint sprig, and lemon peel twist.

RHUBARB SYRUP

Combine 1 cup water, 1 cup fresh or frozen rhubarb pieces (about 1 inch each), and 1 cup sugar in a small saucepan over low heat. Stir often until the sugar has dissolved. Cook over low heat for 15 minutes or until the rhubarb is very soft and is easily broken down when mashed with a spoon. Remove from the heat to cool. Strain through a fine-mesh strainer into a jar, pressing the solids with the back of a spoon. Discard the solids. Store the syrup in the refrigerator for up to 2 weeks. **Makes about 8 ounces (1 cup).**

Fruit Cocktails

Arguably the most popular addition to cocktails—muddled, blended, or juiced—the variety of fruits that may be added to a pitcher, shaker, or glass provide infinite opportunities for magical mixology. You can macerate fruit in a spirit or wine like the Blushing Sangria (*see* page 86), simmer in a syrup to create a boldly flavored sweetener, ferment into vinegar for a Banana Boat Shrub (*see* page 90), or blend as the base for a sparkling sip like The Oh Pear! (*see* page 106). Just know that there are no rules, so play around. Soak a piece of fruit in the spirit of your choice for an hour or two and taste. If you like it, make a cocktail.

CUCUMBER WATER GIN RICKEY

SERVES 1 Cucumber water is so refreshing and is such a nice addition to cocktails. You don't have to use a lot for its distinctive fresh flavor to shine through. Because you blend it skin and all, the juice has a vivid green hue that adds a verdant pop to the drink. One English cucumber (the shrink-wrapped kind) yields anywhere from two-thirds to one cup of cucumber water. Mix it with ginger ale or plain seltzer for a tasty mocktail. Try this method with lemon cucumbers or the melon members of the *Cucurbitaceae* family, such as Crenshaw, Charentais, cantaloupe, honeydew, or watermelon.

1 cucumber ribbon

2 (3-inch) fresh tarragon
   sprigs

3 lime wedges

1 teaspoon sugar

1½ ounce Cucumber Water
   (*recipe follows*)

1 ounce freshly squeezed
   lime juice

2 ounces gin

Club soda

Cucumber slice or spear

Press the cucumber ribbon inside a highball glass in a spiral pattern. Fill the glass with ice.

Muddle 1 tarragon sprig, the lime wedges, and sugar in the bottom of a cocktail shaker. Add the cucumber water, lime juice, gin, and ice and shake vigorously to chill. Strain into the glass. Top with club soda and stir. Garnish with a cucumber slice or spear and the remaining tarragon sprig.

CUCUMBER WATER

Puree 1 English (burpless) cucumber in a high-speed blender, scraping down the sides a time or two, until smooth and blended. Strain through a mesh strainer, pushing solids with the back of a spoon to extract as much liquid as possible. Store in a lidded container in the refrigerator for up to 1 week. **Makes about ¾ cup.**

SMOKY WATERMELON-MEZCAL FRESCA

SERVES 1 Freezing watermelon cubes amps up the chill of this frothy refresher right out of the blender. This drink is a mash-up of a watermelon aqua fresca and a Paloma cocktail that gets its fizz from sweet grapefruit soda—I like to use Squirt or Jarritos. For a less sweet drink, use club soda. To really highlight the smokiness of the mezcal, you might consider grilling ½-inch-thick watermelon wedges over direct high heat for 2 to 3 minutes on each side to develop a nice char. Cool the fruit before cutting it up to freeze.

2 teaspoons smoked sea salt flakes, such as Maldon

½ teaspoon (2 packets) lime crystals, such as True Lime, or fresh lime zest

Grapefruit wedge

1 cup frozen cubed watermelon

4 ounces grapefruit soda or club soda

1½ ounces mezcal

½ ounce freshly squeezed lime juice

Watermelon wedge

Lime wheel

Rim a Collins glass if desired. Fill the glass with ice and set aside.

Make the Smoke-Tart Rim Salt. Combine the sea salt flakes, such as Maldon, and lime crystals or lime zest on a saucer. Rub the lip of a Collins glass with the grapefruit wedge. Invert the glass on the saucer and twist to coat the rim. This will rim about 2 drinks.

Combine the watermelon, grapefruit soda, mezcal, and lime juice in a blender. Blend until smooth. Pour over ice in the prepared glass and garnish with the watermelon wedge and lime wheel.

THE TIKI
BAR BOARD

Tiki drinks have been trending since
the mid-twentieth century, when
Victor Bergeron of Trader Vic's fame
re-created the allure of the islands
in his popular Polynesian-themed
restaurants. He created a fanciful
cocktail menu to complement the
over-the-top, kitschy décor that
seemed straight from the set of
South Pacific, replete with palm
trees, thatched roofs, bamboo
furniture, fishing nets and floats,
and waitresses dressed in sarongs.
Its impact on cocktail culture cannot
be overstated. Classics like the Mai
Tai and Navy Grog were born there,
while appetizers like chicken liver
rumaki, fried shrimp, and egg rolls
were exotic edible enticements. This
food board is inspired by those mid-
century morsels.

*Pineapple
chunks*

*Kiwi
chunks*

*Coconut Dip
for Fruit,*
PAGE 138

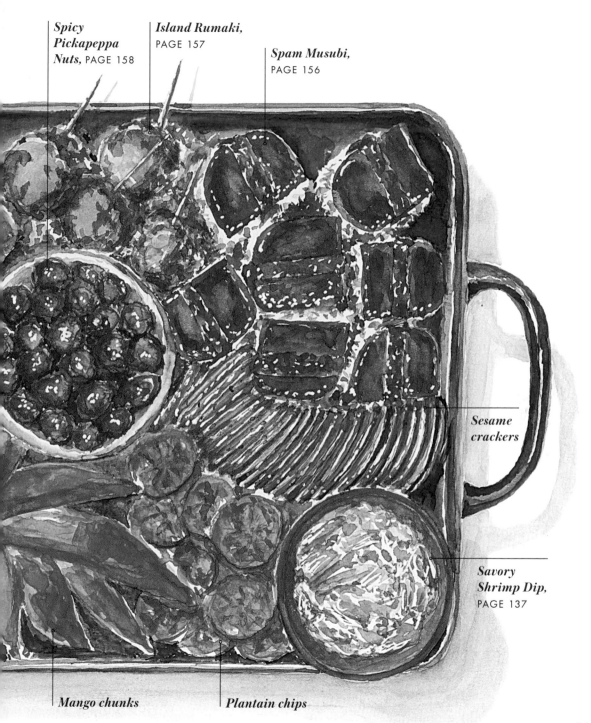

Spicy Pickapeppa Nuts, PAGE 158

Island Rumaki, PAGE 157

Spam Musubi, PAGE 156

Sesame crackers

Savory Shrimp Dip, PAGE 137

Mango chunks

Plantain chips

BLUSHING SANGRIA

SERVES 6 Spanish sangria became popular in the United States when it was introduced at the Spanish Pavilion at the World Fair in 1964. In Spain, recipes remain more or less the same: medium-bodied red wine, fruit, sugar, and often brandy. In the United States, you'll find a host of unexpected variations using a base of vermouth, sake, gin in place of the brandy, and so on. Here, Spanish amontillado sherry adds a nice, dry counterpoint to the aromatic fruit. While there's no need to use the priciest bottle of fine wine here, as in cooking, you should use what you'd enjoy drinking on its own.

1 (750-ml) bottle garnacha rosé wine

4 ounces amontillado sherry

2 ounces Simple Syrup (*see* page 6)

1½ ounces freshly squeezed orange or clementine juice

1 Pink Lady apple, cored and cut into chunks

1 white peach, peeled, pitted, and cut into chunks

1 clementine, sliced and seeded

1 Meyer lemon, sliced and seeded

12 ounces chilled plain seltzer or club soda

18 grapes, frozen

6 citrus wheels

Combine the wine, sherry, syrup, and orange juice in a large pitcher. Add the apple and peach chunks and clementine and lemon slices to the pitcher. Place the pitcher in the refrigerator to chill for at least 2 hours or up to 4.

Stir in the seltzer or club soda just before serving. Add a few frozen grape halves to each stemless wineglass and pour the sangria over, adding a few pieces of the fruit. Garnish each glass with a citrus wheel.

FRUIT SHRUB COCKTAILS

Fruit shrubs are Colonial-era drinking vinegars that have been enjoying renewed popularity. It's a plan-ahead drink that requires letting fruit—flesh, peels, or both—macerate with sugar and water at room temperature so that they begin to break down. Vinegar is then added, and the mixture is left to develop complexity over a few days in the refrigerator before straining. The tart, fruity liquid is then mixed with soda and a spirit for a lively, bright, and very refreshing elixir. Shrubs are a great way to use up overripe, seemingly past-its-prime fruit. You can also add herbs and spices, too. Use neutral white vinegar, wine vinegar, or apple cider vinegar—whatever you like and think will complement the fruit and spirit you are using. If patience is not your virtue, you can approximate a shrub by mixing a fruit simple syrup or cordial like Grenadine (*see* page 7) with equal parts vinegar and then mixing it with your liquor of choice and seltzer to taste.

BANANA BOAT SHRUB
GINGER-ORANGE SHRUB SHANDY
CORDIALLY INVITED SHRUB

BANANA BOAT SHRUB

SERVES 1   I love finding uses for things that often get tossed. Banana peels are a great addition to the compost bin. They are a beneficial fertilizer when buried beneath tomato plants, and I've read that they can shine leather shoes until they gleam. Of all the ways to use the peels, making banana peel vinegar is the most magical of all to me. It's a tart, slightly sweet, versatile ingredient that takes a month or so to ferment in a jar in your pantry. It's surprisingly delicious in salad dressings, sauces, and marinades. You want to use the peels and some fruit from very ripe organic bananas. Do not wash them with soap, rather wipe them down with a damp paper towel to remove any dust or dirt. If you don't want to invest the time to make your own banana vinegar, buy a bottle online, or see a Sneaky Cheat on the next page. That shrub will be something altogether different, yet refreshingly delicious.

3 lime wedges

3 (½-inch) banana slices

1 ounce Spiced Simple Syrup
(*recipe follows*)

1 ounce Banana Vinegar
(*recipe follows*)

1½ ounce rhum agricole or cachaça

Club soda

Lime wheel

Fresh mint sprig

Muddle the lime wedges, banana slices, and syrup in the bottom of a cocktail shaker. Add the vinegar, rhum agricole or cachaça, and ice. Shake vigorously. Strain into a hurricane glass filled with ice. Top with soda and stir to mix. Garnish with a lime wheel and mint sprig.

SPICED SIMPLE SYRUP

Combine ½ cup demerara sugar, 1 teaspoon pumpkin pie spice, and ½ cup water in a small saucepan over low heat. Stir until the sugar dissolves. Remove from the heat to cool. Strain. Stir in ½ ounce overproof vodka. Transfer the syrup to a clean bottle and refrigerate for up to 1 month. **Makes about ¾ cup.**

BANANA VINEGAR

Layer 2 overripe banana peels that have been torn into pieces with 1 sliced banana, 1¼ cup demerara or light brown sugar, and a 1-teaspoon blob of the mother of vinegar from a bottle of unpasteurized apple cider vinegar in a pint-size mason jar. Pour in bottled spring water (not chlorinated water) to about 2 inches from the jar's rim. Cover the jar with a paper towel tightly secured with a rubber band. Place the jar in a cool, dark place for 2 weeks, stirring daily, and then strain. Put the strained liquid in a clean jar. Cover as before and return to the cool, dark place, stirring from time to time until the vinegar is pleasingly tart and acidic. Strain again, reserving the mother to use for a new batch of vinegar. Bottle the banana vinegar in a sterile bottle to use right away, or age it up to 1 year to round out the flavor. **Makes about 1½ cups.**

SNEAKY CHEAT

If you don't want to make your own banana vinegar, this cheat works for a quick banana-flavored shrub. Mix ¾ cup seasoned rice vinegar with ¼ teaspoon banana extract for this drink. Makes ¾ cup.

PANTRY GEM

A bottle of unpasteurized apple cider vinegar with the "mother" floating on the bottom is a staple in my kitchen. Use a bit of that blob as your "starter" for the banana vinegar, or any vinegar you might wish to make. You also can order vinegar mothers on Amazon.

GINGER-ORANGE SHRUB SHANDY

SERVES 1   Shandy shandy shandy, I can't let you go. It's kinda true. This is one refreshing drink that goes down perhaps too easily. Hefeweizen, the yeasty German-style wheat beer that is often served with an orange slice, is an ideal shandy partner for a juicy orange shrub accented with fresh ginger. Shandy comes from the British "shandy gaff," a mix of beer and ginger ale, but now mostly refers to a half-and-half blend of beer and lemonade that is also called a "radler"—German for cyclist. It certainly is a great way to quench your thirst after a long ride or simply a long day.

1 orange slice

3 ounces Ginger-Orange Shrub (*recipe follows*)

1 (12-ounce) bottle wheat beer

Drop an orange slice in the bottom of chilled pint glass. Pour the shrub in the glass. Tilt the glass and slowly top off with the wheat beer.

GINGER-ORANGE SHRUB

Scrub 2 navel oranges and 1 lemon to remove any wax. Coarsely chop the fruit—peel and all—and transfer to a quart-size mason jar. Add ¾ cup sugar and 3 (2-inch-long) thin slices fresh ginger root to the jar. Seal and shake a few times. Refrigerate for 48 hours. Strain through a mesh strainer into a bowl lined with cheesecloth. Gather the corners of the cheesecloth to create a bundle of the solids. Twist the bundle tightly over the bowl to extract as much syrupy citrus juice as possible. Measure the syrup (you should have about 1 cup). Add anywhere from half to an equal amount (to your taste) of your choice of vinegar (white, apple cider, malt, and rice) and transfer the shrub to a clean bottle. Store in the refrigerator up to 2 weeks. **Makes 1½ to 2 cups.**

WHITE VINEGAR

That cheap jug of white vinegar at the supermarket is undervalued. Not only can you use it in cooking and cocktails, but it is a versatile cleaner. Add a cup to your dishwasher to clean and deodorize it. Run it through your coffeemaker to de-scale it. Soak your showerhead in it to remove hard water deposits. Wash ½ cup baking soda with 1 cup white vinegar down a clogged drain to break it up. Mix 1 cup each of white vinegar and water, microwave it for 8 to 10 minutes, and then wipe the condensation away with all the grime. Add 1 to 2 tablespoons to the water in a vase to keep bacteria at bay and extend the life of a bouquet.

CORDIALLY INVITED SHRUB

SERVES 1 When I have a bumper crop of fresh fruit on hand—especially berries—
I often make a batch of fruit cordial. And when you have cordial on hand, I invite you
to use it in countless ways: add a splash to seltzer to create your own soda pop, drizzle
it over ice cream or pancakes, stir it into plain yogurt, use it to imbibe a cake or infuse
cocktails, or mix it with vinegar to create a bright, acidic shrub. I like 3 parts cordial
to 2 parts vinegar, but you can adjust the ratio to suit your tastes. Different fruits lend
themselves to different vinegars and liquors. Try strawberries with rice vinegar and
tequila, blackberries with maple vinegar (available at Whole Foods) and bourbon,
pineapple with apple cider vinegar and rum.

6 fresh or frozen raspberries

1½ ounces Berry Cordial
(*recipe follows*) made with
raspberries

1 ounce champagne vinegar

1½ ounces gin

Champagne or club soda

Lime wheel

Fresh mint sprig

Muddle the raspberries, cordial, vinegar, and gin to a
stemless wineglass and stir to combine. Add ice. Top off
with champagne or club soda. Garnish with a lime wheel
and mint sprig.

BERRY CORDIAL

Combine 1 cup fresh or frozen berries with 1 cup sugar and
cook over medium heat until the sugar melts and the fruit
begins to break down. Reduce heat to a simmer and cook for
20 minutes. Stir in 1 teaspoon freshly squeezed lemon juice
and ½ ounce overproof vodka. Store in a clean bottle in the
refrigerator up to 2 weeks. **Makes about ¾ cup.**

THE
CUPBOARD

3

Beyond the liquor and garnishes behind the cupboard door, there is a motherlode of creative cocktail ingredients hiding in your pantry just waiting to be discovered. Those tea bags can be enlisted to infuse a syrup for the Scottish Lassie (*see* page 120). In a pinch, the potlikker from a can of any kind of shelling beans, not only chickpeas, can be used as a vegan alternative to egg whites in cocktails, as well as provide an interesting flavor note like in the Campfire Brown Derby (*see* page 103). When you crave a summer fruit cocktail in winter or winter fruit cocktail in summer, enlist preserved or canned fruits. An Off-Season Bellini (*see* page 99) made from a puree of canned cling peaches is more than just passable, it's crowd-pleasing when paired with cool-season flavors like vanilla and cinnamon. Shelf-stable staples never sipped so good.

Can-Opener Cocktails

You're likely to find a wine and bottle opener on every bar cart, and perhaps a pointy can tapper for juices, too, but it's time to add a manual can opener to your toolkit. You'll be hard-pressed to make the recipes on the next few pages without one. Canned cranberry sauce moves from holiday table to cocktail shaker for a Thanksgiving Pucker (*see* page 102), a full-bodied sour smash minus the smashing. That dusty can of bone broth purchased for a post-workout restorative can be used in a tastier way. Mix it in a Chuckwagon Stocktail (*see* page 100), a replenishing, iced riff on the bull shot that might numb post-workout pain, too. From broth and beans to squash and fruit, canned goods offer a world of surprising cocktail opportunities.

OFF-SEASON BELLINI

SERVES 6 The Bellini was invented by Giuseppe Cipriani at Harry's Bar in Venice, Italy, in the 1930s and was made only during the season in which fragrant white peaches were at their ripe and juicy best. While peach season is fleeting, you can have your Bellini and drink it too any time of year, thanks to the convenience of canned peaches. Most canned peaches come packed in a mix of peach and pear juices. Since pears ripen in autumn, why not enjoy a spin on this classic cocktail that bridges the seasons?

- 1 (15-ounce) can organic yellow cling peaches in light syrup
- ⅛ teaspoon ground cloves
- ¼ teaspoon pure vanilla extract
- 1 (750-ml) bottle prosecco

Combine the peaches and their syrup in a blender with the cloves and vanilla extract. Blend until smooth.

Spoon about 2 ounces peach puree into the bottoms of six chilled champagne flutes. Top each off with 4 ounces prosecco.

SNEAKY CHEAT

Pureeing canned fruit, juice and all, is a quick way to add fruity flavor to smoothies, iced tea, yogurt, or sauces. You even can make a quick sorbet by freezing unopened cans of fruit. Run them under hot water for a minute before opening the cans at the top and bottom. Press the frozen cylinders of fruit out of the cans. Puree them in a high-speed blender. Transfer to freezer container and re-freeze until ready to scoop.

CHUCKWAGON STOCKTAIL

SERVES 1 There was a time when the broth from a Campbell's soup can was mostly reserved for casseroles and crockpots. Now broth is touted as a cure-all, nutritional powerhouse, hair-and-nail fortifier, muscle-builder, and post-workout recovery drink. Recipes and brands abound. Sip the extracted bone elixir and you are destined for a long, vibrant life it would seem. Whether that's backed by science or completely bunk, bone broth definitely adds flavorful interest to food and drink alike. This smoky, sippable spin on the mid-century Bull Shot is just one mouthwatering example.

2 small lime wedges

2 fresh jalapeño slices, plus 1 for garnish

½ teaspoon Worcestershire sauce

⅛ teaspoon smoked paprika

1 ounce freshly squeezed lime juice

1 ounce vodka, blanco tequila, or mezcal

4 ounces beef bone broth

Beef jerky

Muddle the lime wedges, jalapeño slices, Worcestershire sauce, smoked paprika, and lime juice in the bottom of a double old-fashioned glass. Fill the glass with ice. Add the vodka, tequila, or mezcal, and beef broth. Stir to chill. Garnish the rim with a jalapeño slice and a strip of beef jerky.

THANKSGIVING PUCKER

SERVES 1 Tart and refreshing, cranberry sauce adds viscosity to this drink much like the aquafaba does, giving a substantial heft to the sour taste. The dry spice notes of rye will highlight the orange and sweet-tart cranberry sauce here, while bourbon will add rounded notes of caramel to the mix. Use what you have on hand.

2 ounces rye or bourbon

1 ounce freshly squeezed orange juice

1 ounce organic canned jellied cranberry sauce

1 ounce aquafaba (liquid from a can of chickpeas)

Grated nutmeg

Combine the rye, orange juice, cranberry sauce, and aquafaba in a shaker. Dry shake without ice vigorously. Add ice and shake vigorously again. Strain into a rocks glass with fresh ice. Grate nutmeg over the surface of the drink.

NOTE: When substituting vegan aquafaba for egg whites in cocktails, know that 2 tablespoons chickpea liquid equals 1 large egg white, while 3 tablespoons of the liquid is the equivalent of 1 large whole egg.

CAMPFIRE BROWN DERBY

SERVES 1   My favorite book as a kid was *Baked Beans for Breakfast* by Ruth Chew. I read it over and over until the pages detached from the spine. I found a used copy for my daughters and it captivated me just as much when I read it to them thirty years later. It's about outdoorsy siblings escaping to their family's favorite summertime spot on a lake and living off the land after their parents darted off to Europe without them. They trick their babysitter into believing they've gone off to visit their grandmother . . . actually something easy to get away with back when our every minute wasn't tracked electronically. I wanted to come up with an escape to those long-lost summers in a glass. Since beans have long been considered "a wonderful fruit" (wink wink), I decided to combine the essence of baked beans with a dose of bourbon to conjure campfire cookouts. Bartenders regularly use aquafaba, the bean water from chickpeas, to add body to cocktails. Here the flavorful "potlikker" from a can of baked beans adds body to a variation on the Brown Derby cocktail, while also lending a touch of sweetness and spice. Baked Beans for Cocktail Hour it is! Feel free to omit the bean liquid altogether if the thought is more "no way" than nostalgic. Lose the bacon if you do.

1½ ounces bourbon

1½ ounces liquid from a can of Bush's Best original or vegetarian baked beans

1 ounce freshly squeezed grapefruit juice

¼ ounce maple syrup

2 dashes grapefruit bitters (optional)

Grapefruit peel coin

Cooked bacon slice

Combine the bourbon, bean liquid, grapefruit juice, maple syrup, and bitters, if using, in a shaker with ice. Shake vigorously. Strain into a coupe glass to serve up, or strain into a rocks glass with fresh ice.

Hold a coin-size piece of grapefruit peel over the glass between your finger and thumb with the zest side facing toward the surface of the drink. Hold the flame of a match or lighter an inch from the zest as you squeeze it to express and flame the citrus oils over the drink. Drop the peel in the glass. Garnish the glass with a piece of crisp cooked bacon.

THE WARMING HUT BOARD

I'm lucky to be alive. My parents used to rent skis for my sister and me and drop us off at the foot of the slopes in Red River, Angel Fire, or Taos to ski all day on our own. We were what New Mexicans called "flatlanders," who skied once or twice a year at most. The first time I went skiing I was in fifth grade. I took one half-day lesson and was set free. No one wore helmets or sunscreen. We didn't wear sunglasses, either, to avoid racoon tans. After hours of careening downhill and throwing myself on the ground at the base of the mountain as a stopping technique, I would spend the rest of the day in the warming hut until we got picked up. Over the years, I got my ski legs, thanks to some decent lessons, and became less of a crash-test dummy, but I never stopped loving the warming hut. One of the best is the Lynn Britt Cabin atop Snowmass Mountain, which is more five-star restaurant than hut, but it's worth a stop. This food board is a hybrid of the elevated nibbles you might find there, along with some beloved New Mexico flavors.

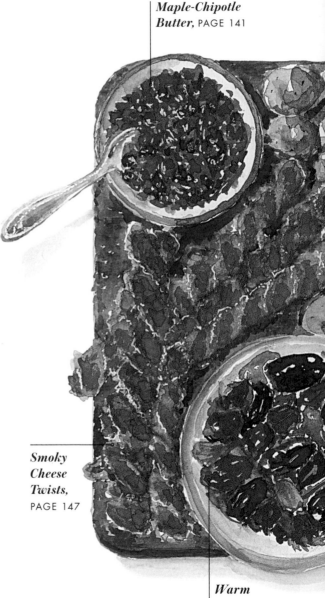

Maple-Chipotle Butter, PAGE 141

Smoky Cheese Twists, PAGE 147

Warm Olive Medley, PAGE 159

Rosemary Corn
Muffins, PAGE 148

Blue corn
tortilla chips

Picadillo,
PAGE 143

Dried Chile Salsa,
PAGE 140

Marinated
Queso Fresco,
PAGE 139

THE OH PEAR!

SERVES A PAIR Use the pear cup you might put in a lunchbox to make the base for this not-too-sweet autumnal tipple. Add more honey for a sweeter drink.

1 (4-ounce) diced pear fruit cup in fruit juice

½ teaspoon honey

Juice of ½ lemon

¼ teaspoon ground ginger

2 ounces bourbon

6 ounces chilled ginger ale

Candied ginger

Lemon wheel

Empty the entire contents of the pear cup into a blender. Add the honey, lemon juice, ground ginger, and bourbon. Blend until smooth. Add ice to 2 double old-fashioned or stemless wineglasses. Pour 4 ounces of the puree in each glass. Top each with 3 ounces of the ginger ale. Stir for 20 seconds to mix and chill. Garnish with candied ginger and a lemon wheel.

LUSCIOUS CUPBOARD COCKTAILS

Dreamy, creamy cocktails make adults feel like kids in an ice cream shop. The brain lights up with activity when creamy liquids or fats hit the tongue, and when sweet registers on the tastebuds, it might as well be the Fourth of July in there. These are meant to be indulgent, occasional drinks. The Pumpkin Pie Alexander (*see* page 110) is a festive way to end a fall dinner party, while the Mandarin Painkiller (*see* page 111) and Green Batida (*see* page 111) are decadent summertime refreshers that would be right at home in the cupholder of a lounge chair by the pool or on the beach.

PUMPKIN PIE ALEXANDER
MANDARIN PAINKILLER
GREEN BATIDA

PUMPKIN PIE ALEXANDER

SERVES 1 The classic Alexander was made with gin, chocolate liqueur, and cream, though brandy Alexanders quickly became more popular, overshadowing the OG. It's a cocktail that tastes like a festive fireside extra, meant to celebrate a holiday or special occasion . . . if only the close of a fine evening. To give the cocktail an autumnal spin, I traded the chocolate for pumpkin and infused it with almond-scented amaretto—or try it with hazelnut-infused Frangelico or pecan-based praline liqueur. Mix these ingredients in a mug without ice and stir in 4 ounces hot coffee for a fortifying hot toddy that is ideal for sipping while wrangling trick-or-treaters.

1 tablespoon canned pumpkin

1 ounce cognac

1 ounce amaretto, Frangelico, or praline liqueur

1 ounce heavy cream

Pumpkin pie spice

Combine the pumpkin puree, cognac, liqueur, and heavy cream in a shaker with ice. Shake vigorously and strain into a chilled coupe glass. Garnish with a sprinkle of pumpkin pie spice.

PANTRY GEM

Canned pumpkin is delicious in pie, but also in ravioli, ice cream, layered with custard in a trifle, or whipped into a smoothie. A spoonful is also a recommended addition to a dog's food when they have tummy woes. Know that canned "pure pumpkin" is actually not pumpkin at all, but one or a blend of several winter squash varieties more closely related to the butternut.

MANDARIN PAINKILLER

SERVES 1 The Painkiller is a spin on the creamy piña colada that was created at the Soggy Dollar Bar in the British Virgin Islands and then trademarked by Pusser's Rum in the 1980s. It is usually made with orange juice, though here a puree of canned mandarin orange segments lend even more body and concentrated flavor to this tropical standard.

1½ ounce dark rum

1½ ounces Mandarin Orange Puree (*recipe follows*)

3 ounces unsweetened pineapple juice

1 ounce canned coconut cream

Pineapple wedge

Pinch ground allspice

Combine the rum, Mandarin Orange Puree, pineapple juice, and coconut cream in a shaker with ice. Shake vigorously. Strain over fresh ice in a hurricane glass. Garnish with a pineapple wedge and a pinch of ground allspice.

MANDARIN ORANGE PUREE

Blend 1 (8.25-ounce) can mandarin orange in light syrup in a blender until pureed. Store in a clean jar for 1 week. **Makes about ⅔ cup.**

GREEN BATIDA

SERVES 1 The Batida is a Brazilian cachaça cocktail made with fruit juice and sugar but can also be a Portuguese milkshake. This cocktail combines the two. It gets its richness from a blend of avocado and canned coconut milk and its flavorful sweetness from the warm-spiced falernum syrup. Try this with basil in place of the mint for an equally delicious creamy herb-scented cocktail.

⅛ avocado, peeled

3 fresh mint leaves

1 ounce Cheater's Falernum (*see page 8*)

1 ounce freshly squeezed lime juice

½ ounce canned coconut milk

2 ounces cachaça or white rum

Pinch toasted shredded coconut

Lime zest curl

Fresh mint sprig

Muddle the avocado, mint leaves, and falernum in a cocktail shaker. Add the lime juice, coconut milk, cachaça, and ice. Shake vigorously. Strain over fresh ice in a rocks glass. Garnish with a pinch of toasted coconut, a lime zest curl, and a mint sprig.

Leaf, Bean &
Spice Drawer Sips

By now, if you've flipped through this book and made a few cocktails, you know that most any category of ingredient can find its way into a delectable drink. Condiments, canned goods, herbs, and produce have as much of a place in cocktail crafting as they do in cooking. Dehydrated and dry ingredients are no exception. In the recipes that follow, they play a more prominent role. Bold spices shine with rum in a Golden Milk Coquito (*see* page 113), gin in the fennel-tinged Final Say (*see* page 119), and bourbon in an exotic Buzzed Café Cassis (*see* page 125). White rice, cinnamon, and cacao nibs collide with tequila in a boozy Horchata Oaxacan (*see* page 115). Matcha tea escapes the mug, infusing the gingery Pagoda Fizz (*see* page 116) with earthy flavor while Lady Grey tea puts the outspoken scotch in a quieter place in the sublime Scottish Lassie (*see* page 120).

GOLDEN MILK COQUITO

SERVES 1   Golden milk is an ancient Indian elixir from the Ayurvedic tradition. Ayurveda is the combination of two words: *ayur* (life) and *veda* (knowledge) and is a system of a natural medicine that seeks to balance mind, body, and spirit through the practice of purification, diet, meditation, massage, yoga, and natural remedies. Golden milk is a turmeric, black pepper, spice, and warm milk mixture that is drunk for its anti-inflammatory, healing properties. Consider it the chicken soup of any Indian mother's kitchen. She likely wouldn't spike it with rum, of course, but this marriage of golden milk and the Puerto Rican nog called *coquito* proves that cocktails without borders are a thing of beauty. Be very careful when using ground or fresh turmeric. It stains whatever it touches.

1 tablespoon Turmeric Tea Base (*recipe follows*)

Pinch ground cinnamon

1 ounce sweetened condensed milk

3 ounces canned coconut milk

1½ ounces white rum

Pinch of ground turmeric

Cinnamon stick

Combine the tea base, cinnamon, sweetened condensed milk, coconut milk, and rum in a shaker with ice. Shake vigorously. Strain over fresh ice in a rocks glass. Garnish with a pinch of turmeric and a cinnamon stick.

TURMERIC TEA BASE

Whisk together ½ cup honey, 3 teaspoons ground turmeric, 1 teaspoon ground ginger, 1 teaspoon finely grated orange zest, and ½ teaspoon finely ground black pepper in a small jar until incorporated. Seal and keep in a cool, dark place for up to 2 weeks. Add 1 teaspoon Turmeric Tea Base to 8 ounces hot water for tea, or hot milk for golden milk, or add it to the shaker for this cocktail. **Makes ½ cup.**

HORCHATA OAXACAN

SERVES 1 Plan ahead for this one, but it's worth the wait. Lots of bartenders infuse entire bottles of liquor, but I like to start with a small 375-ml bottle or even just 8 ounces to see if I like the flavor that the infusion imparts before I commit to making a big batch. Know that even using regular tequila here makes a delicious drink.

- 2 ounces Cacao Nib–Infused Tequila (*recipe follows*) or mezcal
- 1 ounce Kahlúa
- 2 ounces Homemade Horchata (*recipe follows*)
- Pinch of ground cinnamon
- Cinnamon stick

Combine the tequila or mezcal, Kahlúa, and horchata in a shaker with ice. Shake vigorously. Strain into an ice-filled rocks glass. Garnish with a pinch of ground cinnamon and a cinnamon stick.

HOMEMADE HORCHATA

Combine 1 cup long-grain white rice, 1 cinnamon stick broken into pieces, 3½ cups very hot water, and 1 (14-ounce) can sweetened condensed milk in a mixing bowl. Stir well to incorporate. Cover and refrigerate overnight. Transfer to a high-speed blender and, starting on low speed and increasing to high speed, blend for 2 to 3 minutes until smooth. Strain through a mesh strainer to remove any grainy bits. Stir in 4 cups whole milk. Store in a 2½-quart pitcher in the refrigerator up to 1 week. **Makes about 9 cups.**

VARIATION

For a dairy-free Homemade Horchata, substitute 1 cup Simple Syrup (*see* page 6) for the sweetened condensed milk and 2 cups dairy-free milk for the whole milk.

CACAO NIB–INFUSED TEQUILA

Toast 3 tablespoons raw (not roasted) cacao nibs in a small dry skillet over medium heat for 3 minutes until their cloudy exterior becomes dark, glossy, and fragrant. Transfer the nibs to a plate to cool. Lightly crush them with the bottom of a rocks glass. Place the crushed nibs in a jar and pour 8 ounces tequila over them and seal. Shake the jar. Leave it in a cool, dark place, shaking a couple times daily for 5 days. Strain through a mesh strainer lined with cheesecloth into a clean bottle. Use within 6 months. **Makes 1 cup.**

PAGODA FIZZ

SERVES 1 Earthy vegetal matcha tea combines with the crisp juniper notes of gin in this classic fizz accented with fresh ginger. It has an eye-opening dose of caffeine, too, so if you're sensitive, this one is best sipped earlier in the evening.

½ teaspoon finely grated ginger root or ½ teaspoon ground ginger

½ teaspoon matcha tea powder

2 ounces gin

1 ounce freshly squeezed lemon juice

1 ounce Simple Syrup (*see* page 6)

1 ounce heavy cream

1 large egg white

Club soda

Pinch of ground ginger

Candied ginger

Combine the grated ginger, matcha tea, gin, lemon juice, simple syrup, cream, and egg white in a shaker. Dry shake without ice. Add ice and shake vigorously for 2 minutes to emulsify the ingredients.

Add 1 ounce club soda to the chilled glass and strain the cocktail into the glass. Top with more soda so that the raft of foam rises just above the rim of the glass. Sprinkle with a pinch of ground ginger and garnish with a skewer of candied ginger.

FINAL SAY

SERVES 1   This is a riff on the Last Word, a Prohibition cocktail made with gin, green Chartreuse, maraschino liqueur, and lime juice. Here, the syrup from a jar of maraschino cherries and another made from fresh fennel and crushed fennel seeds brings the sweet, herbal notes of the classic cocktail with less of an investment.

1½ ounces gin

½ ounce syrup from jar of Luxardo maraschino cherries

½ ounce Fennel Simple Syrup (*recipe follows*)

1 ounce freshly squeezed lemon juice

2 to 3 Luxardo maraschino cherries

Fennel stalk with fronds (optional)

Combine the gin, cherry syrup, Fennel Simple Syrup, and lemon juice in a shaker with ice. Shake vigorously. Strain into a Nick and Nora glass and garnish with a skewer of cherries and a fennel stalk, if desired.

FENNEL SIMPLE SYRUP

Combine ½ cup sugar, ½ cup water, and ½ cup chopped green fennel stalks (reserve the bulb and fronds for cooking and garnishing), and ½ teaspoon bruised fennel seeds in a small saucepan over medium heat until the sugar dissolves and the syrup begins to simmer. Remove the pan from heat and let the fennel steep in the syrup for 30 minutes as it cools. Stir in ¼ ounce overproof vodka and strain into a clean bottle. Refrigerate for up to 1 month. **Makes about ¾ cup.**

SCOTTISH LASSIE

SERVES 1 Lady Grey Tea is a bergamot and black tea blend that is milder in flavor than Earl Grey, and with orange and lemon peel added. The flavors meld beautifully with peaty scotch and the rich, fruity notes of the liqueur. The egg white tames the boozy bite and fuses them all together with each velvety sip. If you think you don't like scotch, let this be your gateway gulp.

1½ ounces blended scotch

½ ounce crème de cassis

½ ounce Lady Grey Tea Syrup (*recipe follows*)

1 large egg white

Lemon peel coin

Combine the scotch, crème de cassis, syrup, and egg white in a shaker without ice. Dry shake for 30 seconds. Fill halfway with ice and shake vigorously to chill. Strain into a chilled coupe or rocks glass.

Hold a coin-size piece of lemon peel over the glass between your finger and thumb with the zest side facing toward the surface of the drink. Hold the flame of a match or lighter an inch from the zest as you squeeze it to express and flame the citrus oils over the drink. Drop the peel in the glass.

LADY GREY TEA SYRUP

Boil ½ cup water and 1 Lady Grey tea bag in a small saucepan over high heat. Remove from the heat and add ½ cup sugar and stir until it dissolves. Transfer the syrup to a clean bottle and refrigerate for up to 1 week. **Makes about ½ cup.**

THE CONTINENTAL LOUNGE BOARD

If you have a chance to visit or stay at the TWA Hotel inside JFK Airport in New York, I highly recommend it. It's definitely a walk back in time. From furniture and finishes to food and drink, it is vintage in all the right ways at every turn. My experience during a long layover there inspired this food board of retro cocktail-hour nibbles, which would be equally fitting on the set of *Madmen*, enjoyed with the show's symbolic Old Fashioned or a Dirty Dry Martini (*see* page 35).

Caramelized shallots,
SEE PAGE 160

Bagel Chips,
PAGE 149

Beluga Lentil "Caviar,"
PAGE 160

Smoked salmon

Black Pepper Crème Fraîche, PAGE 142

Capers

Stuffed Mushrooms, PAGE 161

Pistachios

Diced red onion

BUZZED CAFÉ CASSIS

SERVES 1   In Morocco, liquor isn't quite illegal, but it is frowned upon. Coffee and tea are the libation mainstays. While most Moroccans aren't boozing up their cups, hotel bars that cater to tourists do serve wine and spirits. This warm tipple might not be traditional, but its exotic flavors sure taste good. Ras El Hanout is a popular spice blend that translates to "top of the shop" in reference to the high-quality spices used in the blend, which can contain 20 to 100 spices or more. Shopkeepers and cooks all over Morocco keep their signature recipes a closely guarded secret. This boozy, spiced coffee would be considered *mazboutah*, or medium sweet, unless you add the sugar cubes, which would make it very sweet, or *hilweh*.

1½ ounces bourbon

½ ounce Honey Syrup (*see* page 7) or 1 teaspoon honey

1 tablespoon Ras El Hanout Coffee Blend (*recipe follows*)

4 ounces boiling water

2 ounces scalded or steamed milk

Pinch ground cardamom

Cinnamon stick

Sugar cubes

Combine the bourbon and syrup in a warm heatproof mug. Set a single-cup coffee percolator lined with a coffee filter over the mug (alternatively line a small mesh strainer with cheesecloth). Add the Ras El Hanout Coffee Blend. Pour the boiling water over the coffee. Let it drip into the mug. Top with the hot milk. Serve immediately with a sprinkle of ground cardamom, a cinnamon stick, and sugar cubes on the side, for sweetening further, to taste.

RAS EL HANOUT COFFEE BLEND

Combine ½ teaspoon ground white pepper, ½ teaspoon ground ginger, ½ teaspoon ground nutmeg, ½ teaspoon ground cinnamon, ¼ teaspoon ground cardamom, ¼ teaspoon ground allspice, ¼ teaspoon ground anise seed, ⅛ teaspoon ground cloves, and ⅛ teaspoon cayenne to 1 cup freshly ground Arabica coffee beans (ground medium-coarse for a percolator). Stir well to distribute the spices throughout the coffee. Store in an airtight container and use within 2 weeks. **Makes 1 generous cup.**

FOOD
BOARD
BASICS

4

Several of the recipes that follow are perhaps too simple even to be called recipes—Warm Olive Medley, anyone?—but it's simplicity that gives the home cook and maison mixologist the freedom to finesse and have more time with their guests. The twist of a jar lid or opening of a can should be celebrated, not maligned, in our crazy, busy world. Of course if you have the raw ingredients, time, and desire to make pesto from scratch, do it, but there is no shame in turning to store-bought if it's good or you embellish it to suit your tastes. After all, if you're going to the trouble of making Stuffed Mushrooms (*see* page 161) for a crowd, then filling them with prepared pesto is a sneaky cheat that gets you to the finish line a hop, skip, and a jump faster.

All of the recipes here appear on the themed food boards throughout this book, but each is a tasty staple that can be paired and served myriad ways. Rather than group them with the recipes that they are paired with on the food boards, they are divided into categories by recipe type. Hopefully, that makes it easier to mix things up and create cocktail-hour nibble combos that pique your interest and whet appetites.

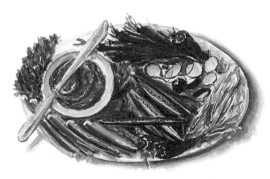

Dips, Drizzles
& Spreads

A great dip or spread is like the comfort food of cocktail hour, plus
most are easily made ahead and kept chilled until serving time.
Whether it's a boldly flavored cheese ball, a hot dip for a crudité platter,
or a rich compound butter to slather on a hot muffin, turn to your
fridge and pantry for an abundant supply of ingredients to whip up,
fold in, or spoon on. No food board is complete without one (or two).

BEER CHEESE SPREAD

MAKES ABOUT 3 CUPS This Clark County, Kentucky, classic is meant to have a sharp, spicy bite and pronounced beer flavor. Shred the cheese yourself for the best texture. Serve this with celery sticks, bell pepper strips, kettle chips, crackers, or crusty bread, whatever your preferred vehicle for getting this in your mouth. This recipe makes a large batch, but it freezes surprisingly well, so enjoy this now and save some for later. It's also a great served between two slices of rye bread with lettuce and a slice of tomato.

1 pound block extra-sharp cheddar, shredded

1 pound block white cheddar, shredded

4 ounces cream cheese, softened

1 large shallot, peeled and minced

4 large garlic cloves, peeled and minced

¼ cup sliced green onions

½ teaspoon ground mustard

½ teaspoon cayenne

1 teaspoon kosher salt

1 teaspoon freshly ground black pepper

1 tablespoon hot sauce

½ teaspoon Worcestershire sauce

6 ounces brown ale (*see Pantry Gem below*)

1 cup coarsely chopped toasted pecans (optional)

Combine the cheeses, shallot, garlic, green onions, ground mustard, cayenne, salt, pepper, hot sauce, and Worcestershire in a food processor fitted with the metal blade. Pulse several times to blend. Slowly pour the ale through the food tube with the processor running until the cheese is smooth and creamy.

Transfer to a serving bowl, cover, and chill for at least 4 hours before serving, to allow the flavors to come together. Divide the cheese in half, form into 2 balls, and roll each ball in chopped pecans, if desired. The cheese may be served cold or at room temperature.

PANTRY GEM
Lazy Magnolia Nut Brown Ale is delicious for sipping, but its dark nuttiness is surprisingly tasty as the starring ingredient in this beer cheese.

PIMENTO CHEESE

MAKES 2½ CUPS There are as many renditions of pimento cheese in the South as there are mosquitos. We all are partial to a recipe or two. One steadfast rule is to shred the cheese yourself for the best texture. Some say you must use Duke's mayonnaise, while others demand that Hellmann's is the only way to go. Choose whichever you like. When I don't make my own, I head to a little takeout casserole place in my neighborhood fittingly called Dish'n It Out. I've never asked for their recipe, but I've picked it apart while eating it right from the container. It's mostly well-seasoned shredded cheese and pimentos bound with mayo, but it is dotted with chopped walnuts and capers, too. The briny and crunchy are nice additions. I use toasted pecans instead. I've always liked a little something pickled in the mix too, so often I'll add a bit of whatever jar I have open in the fridge: chopped pickled okra, manzanilla olives, peperoncini, peppadews, cocktail onions, dill pickle relish, or cornichons.

1 (8-ounce) block cheddar

1 (4-ounce) block Gouda

½ cup mayonnaise

1 (4-ounce) jar pimentos, drained

¼ cup chopped toasted pecans

1 tablespoon capers, chopped

½ teaspoon cayenne

Shred the cheese using the large holes of a box grater or the shredding attachment of a food processor.

Combine the mayonnaise, pimentos, pecans, capers, and cayenne in a bowl and stir to combine. Fold in the shredded cheese a bit at time until incorporated.

Refrigerate for at least 4 hours before serving, to allow the flavors to come together.

CREAMY REMOULADE

MAKES ABOUT 1½ CUPS   Remoulade is both a sauce and a salad. This is the sauce—a French mayonnaise-based sauce with bold flavor and myriad uses. Also French, the salad is a grated or julienned raw celery root, or celeriac, slaw that is also delicious. But again, this is not that. Serve this as a quenching sauce for the Cajun Chicken Pops (*see* page 153).

½ cup mayonnaise

½ cup sour cream

Grated zest and juice of 2 lemons

1 tablespoon whole-grain mustard

1 tablespoon sliced chives

1 tablespoon chopped fresh tarragon

2 tablespoons chopped fresh parsley

1 tablespoon hot sauce

1 teaspoon Worcestershire sauce

½ teaspoon celery salt

¼ teaspoon freshly ground black pepper

Combine the mayonnaise, sour cream, lemon zest and juice, mustard, chives, tarragon, parsley, hot sauce, Worcestershire, celery salt, and pepper in a bowl and mix well. Refrigerate for at least 1 hour, to allow the flavors to come together.

FROMAGE FORT

MAKES ABOUT 1 CUP I'd missed out on studying abroad, so a couple years after college I left my job in DC to work the vendange—the annual grape harvest—in Bordeaux at a vineyard called Domaine de Chevalier in order to satisfy and finance my wanderlust. From there, I moved on to Aix-en-Provence, where I worked as a nanny for a time. The mother of the kids I looked after was an amazing cook who awed me with her ability to turn the simplest ingredients into something delicious. She would gather the odds, ends, and remnants from our cheese plates and then whirl them in a food processor with a few splashes of vermouth or wine from her glass. If the mix was too strongly flavored (*fromage fort* does translate to "strong cheese"), she'd mellow things with a knob or two of butter and a smattering of fresh herbs, and then transfer the mix to a ramekin. This was spread on toast, set out with ham and a baguette for a delicious lunch, or part of the post-dinner cheese course.

3 tablespoons dry vermouth or white wine

1 small shallot, sliced

1 small garlic clove, coarsely chopped

Salt and freshly ground black pepper

½ pound cheese remnants

¼ cup loosely packed tender herb leaves, such as chervil, tarragon, or parsley

4 tablespoons softened French butter, such as Plugra (optional)

Combine the vermouth or wine with the shallot and garlic in a small bowl. Add a pinch of salt and a few grindings of black pepper. Set aside for 10 minutes to macerate.

Toss the cheese and herbs into the bowl of a food processor fitted with the metal blade. Add the vermouth mixture and process until smooth. Taste and add the butter if the flavor is too strong. Season with more salt and pepper, if needed.

RUSSIAN DRESSING

MAKES ABOUT 1 CUP   Finding a bottle of Russian dressing next to the
Thousand Island or French dressing on grocery store shelves was much easier
a half century ago. Luckily, it's a condiment mash-up that's super easy to make
and the classic condiment for a Reuben (see page 151), but it's also terrific as
a sauce for dunking chilled cooked shrimp or dressing an iceberg wedge.
Fun fact: The same dressing in Germany is called "American dressing."

¾ cup mayonnaise

¼ cup ketchup

1 tablespoon grated white
   onion

2 teaspoons prepared
   horseradish

¼ teaspoon dry mustard

½ teaspoon Worcestershire
   sauce

½ teaspoon cayenne

Combine the mayonnaise, ketchup, onion, horseradish, dry
mustard, Worcestershire sauce, and cayenne in a small bowl.
Store in a jar in the refrigerator for up to 2 weeks.

ROASTED RED GRAPES

MAKES ABOUT 1½ CUPS   When the grapes in your fridge are starting
to shrivel, make this easy recipe. It's delicious spooned over a grilled pork chop,
tucked with sliced turkey into a pita, or served in a bowl with a spoon as a sweet
counterpoint to a selection of cheeses. Try this with green grapes, purple grapes,
or muscadines and scuppernongs, too.

1 bunch seedless red grapes
   (about 2½ cups)

1 tablespoon extra-virgin
   olive oil

1 tablespoon chopped fresh
   rosemary

¼ teaspon kosher salt

½ teaspoon fresh thyme
   leaves

2 tablespoon toasted pine
   nuts (optional)

Preheat the oven to 400°F. Line a rimmed baking sheet with
a piece of parchment paper.

   Rinse the grapes in a colander and dry them well. Toss
them in a bowl with the olive oil, rosemary, and salt. Spread
in an even layer on the prepared pan and roast for 12 minutes,
stirring halfway through, until caramelized and bursting.
Transfer to a bowl and sprinkle with thyme leaves and the
toasted pine nuts, if desired.

BROWN BUTTER BAGNA CAUDA

MAKES ¾ CUP *Bagna cauda* translates to "hot bath," and that's what this is—an addictively savory hot dunk tailor-made for a platter of raw, steamed, or roasted vegetables. Cardoons are a classic dipper, but tender Steamed Baby Artichokes (*see* page 155) are another worthy match. Try this spooned over grilled radicchio or tossed with a salad of sturdy greens. The classic recipe is just olive oil, garlic, and anchovies, but I like the rich nuttiness that brown butter adds, along with the vibrancy of a splash of acidic lemon juice or vinegar.

½ stick unsalted butter

½ cup olive oil

4 large garlic cloves, sliced

8 oil-packed anchovy fillets

2 teaspoons lemon juice or white wine vinegar (optional)

Melt the butter in a small skillet over medium heat, shaking the pan from time to time until the foam subsides and the milk solids turn golden. Remove the pan from heat. The butter will continue to brown a bit as it cools.

Heat the olive oil and garlic in a small saucepan over low heat. Cook slowly, stirring often, until soft and golden, about 30 minutes. Add the anchovies and stir with a wooden spoon, breaking them up. Remove from heat and add the brown butter and the lemon juice or vinegar, if using. For a less chunky sauce, pulse the mixture with an immersion blender a time or two. Serve warm.

PANTRY GEM

Don't snub your nose at anchovies. If you don't already, you will appreciate them once you realize all the wonderful ways they can elevate your cooking. Think of anchovies like that bottle of Worcestershire, soy, or fish sauce that you keep in your cupboard. These gems of the sea add that boost of umami you expect in puttanesca sauce, Caesar dressing, pizza, quiche, compound butter . . . and the list goes on. Whether you buy oil-packed or salt-packed, just buy them!

SAVORY SHRIMP DIP

MAKES ABOUT 3 CUPS This dip is also terrific made with lump crabmeat or crawfish tailmeat in place of the shrimp. Amp up the spiciness by upping the cayenne or adding more minced jalapeño to the mix. Though any size of peeled, cooked shrimp can be used here, I keep a bag of tiny cooked salad shrimp in my freezer for salads and dips like this because it makes chopping so much quicker.

1 (8-ounce) block cream cheese, softened

2 tablespoons freshly grated Parmigiano-Reggiano

3 green onions, thinly sliced

2 celery stalks, thinly sliced

1 jalapeño pepper, minced

½ teaspoon kosher salt

¼ teaspoon cayenne

1 tablespoon finely grated lemon zest

2 tablespoons freshly squeezed lemon juice

1 (3.5-ounce) jar capers, drained

1 pound frozen peeled cooked shrimp, thawed and chopped

Combine the cream cheese, Parmigiano-Reggiano, green onions, celery, jalapeño, salt, cayenne, lemon zest, lemon juice, capers, and shrimp in a bowl, mixing well. Place a piece of plastic wrap directly on the surface of the dip and chill for at least 4 hours before serving.

SNEAKY CHEAT
Flavored cream cheeses are a convenient option to use here. Check out blends at your local deli or look for one of the many Philadelphia Cream Cheese flavors like spicy jalapeño, cracked pepper & olive oil, or chive & onion, to boost the flavor of this dip right out of the gate.

COCONUT DIP FOR FRUIT

MAKES ABOUT 1⅔ CUPS Chill the canned coconut cream and mixing bowl and beaters for at least four hours or overnight for whipping success. The touch of salt really brings out the flavors here, and I highly recommend the cayenne, which highlights the fruit in that way that a bit of chile and lime make watermelon taste sweeter.

1 (13.5-ounce) can coconut cream, chilled

¼ cup powdered sugar

½ teaspoon lime zest

1 tablespoon freshly squeezed lime juice

3 tablespoons minced fresh mint (from ½-ounce bunch)

⅛ teaspoon kosher salt

Pinch cayenne (optional)

Open the chilled coconut cream with a can opener and spoon the layer of thick cream into the chilled mixing bowl, leaving the liquid behind; reserve the liquid.

Beat the cream on low speed to loosen, about 30 seconds. Sift the powdered sugar over the cream and add the lime zest, juice, mint, salt, and cayenne. Beat on medium speed until thick and creamy and it reaches the consistency of Greek yogurt. Transfer to a bowl and use right away or refrigerate to thicken further. Serve with any fruit of your choice.

PANTRY GEM

For drinks and dishes, coconut milk and cream are super versatile. Whether you're mixing a creamy tiki drink, making curry for a crowd, or need a vegan substitute for dairy, these are tasty essentials to have on hand. Think of coconut milk and coconut cream like Simple Syrup and Rich Simple Syrup (*see* page 6). Coconut milk is made from a 1:1 ratio of coconut meat to water with a texture similar to cow's milk, while coconut cream is its more substantial cousin made with a 4:1 ratio of coconut meat to water, giving it a thick, rich consistency.

MARINATED QUESO FRESCO

SERVES 6 This marinated salty, crumbly Mexican cheese is very similar to marinated feta. It is delicious served with chips and a roasted chile salsa, tossed in a green salad, or used as a flavorful finishing cheese for tacos or enchiladas. The smoky almonds are a nice, crunchy counterpoint to the cheese.

1 garlic clove, minced

2 tablespoons white wine vinegar

2 tablespoons honey

1 tablespoon freshly squeezed orange juice

Kosher salt

½ teaspoon red pepper flakes

¼ cup plus 2 tablespoons olive oil

1 (10-ounce) wheel queso fresco

1½ tablespoons Mexican oregano

4 ounces smoked almonds, chopped

Place the garlic in a jar with the vinegar, honey, orange juice, salt, and red pepper flakes. Seal tightly, shake to mix, and set aside for 10 minutes. Add the oil to the jar, seal tightly, and shake vigorously to emulsify.

Place the wheel of queso fresco in a zip-top plastic bag and seal. Use your fingers to break up the cheese in the bag into a mix of bigger chunks and smaller crumbles. Transfer the cheese to a bowl. Add the oregano, almonds, and vinaigrette and toss well to combine. Cover and refrigerate the cheese for at least 4 hours to let the flavors come together.

PANTRY GEM
Many cooks turn to dried Italian oregano when a recipe calls for Mexican oregano, but the two herbs come from entirely different plants. Italian oregano is a member of the mint family, while Mexican oregano is a relative of vervain and has a strong, earthy flavor with pronounced citrusy notes and it stands up well to bold-flavored or spicy dishes. Marjoram is a better swap for Mexican oregano than the dried Italian variety. But try to stock up on the real thing.

DRIED CHILE SALSA

MAKES ABOUT 1½ CUPS Each summer I beat the heat by spending time at my family's cabin at 7,500 feet in the Rocky Mountains of northeastern New Mexico, and each summer I have a hoarder's compulsion to stock up on every variety of Mexican dried chile I can put my hands on. I bring bags of them home. Once opened, they often get separated from their labels, so I don't always know what's what. I'll have chile de árbols, anchos, chipotles, guajillos, cascabels, and New Mexico red chiles. Often I just grab a mix of them all to make this salsa, which means no two batches taste alike, but I am all for spicy surprises. This is terrific with chips, mixed with mayo for a zippy sauce, or slathered on chicken thighs, pork shoulder, or chuck roast before braising to shred for tacos.

6 tablespoons vegetable oil

3 ounces (about ⅓ cup) mixed dried chiles

8 garlic cloves, peeled

½ cup chopped red onion

2 tablespoons Mexican oregano or marjoram (*see page 139*)

1 teaspoon kosher salt

1 tablespoon sugar

2 tablespoons red wine vinegar

1 cup hot water

½ cup chopped fresh cilantro

Heat 1 tablespoon of the oil in a large cast-iron skillet over medium heat. Add the chiles and garlic cloves and cook, turning occasionally, until the chiles puff up and become fragrant and the garlic is brown, about 5 minutes. Transfer the chiles to a bowl and set the garlic aside. Cover the chiles with boiling water and let soak for 15 minutes to soften.

Meanwhile, add another tablespoon of the oil to the pan and add the onion, oregano, and salt and cook until the onion is soft and golden, 4 to 5 minutes. Remove from the heat.

Drain the chiles and remove the stems, seeds, and veins. Transfer the chiles, garlic, and onion mixture, with the sugar, vinegar, and hot water to a blender and puree until smooth.

Heat the remaining ¼ cup oil in a large skillet over medium heat. Add the puree and cook, stirring with a wooden spoon until the mixture thickens and begins to stick to the pan, about 10 minutes. Taste and season with additional salt and a splash of vinegar, to taste. Remove from heat and transfer to a bowl. Thin with a bit of hot water, if desired. Stir in the cilantro.

MAPLE-CHIPOTLE BUTTER

MAKES 1 (4-OUNCE) LOG Compound butter is another terrific recipe to make and keep in your freezer. It's a great way to use up a bumper crop of herbs, citrus zest, spices from the spice drawer, anchovies, olives, capers, or even the last bits of a jar of tapenade, caponata, harissa, or pesto. Having a log or two on hand means you have a tasty spread for warm bread, a pat or two to melt on top of a piece of grilled fish or meat, and a wonderful flavor enhancer to enrich a pan sauce when whisked in at the end of cooking. This butter is my go-to slather for the Rosemary Corn Muffins (*see* page 148), but it elevates plain old store-bought cornbread, too.

1 stick unsalted butter, softened

3 canned chipotles in adobo, minced (about 1½ tablespoons)

1 teaspoon maple syrup

¼ teaspoon lime juice

¼ teaspoon smoked sea salt flakes, such as Maldon

Combine the butter, chipotles, maple syrup, and lime juice in a small bowl. Crush the sea salt flakes between your fingertips and sprinkle over the butter. Mix to combine. Transfer the butter to a sheet of parchment paper and roll into a log shape, twisting the ends like a Tootsie Roll. Chill for several hours or overnight to let the flavors come together and the butter to firm up.

Compound butter will keep for 2 weeks in the refrigerator and up to a year in the freezer sealed in airtight freezer bags.

HOME-CHURNED CRÈME FRAÎCHE

MAKES 1 CUP It's nice to know how to make buttermilk, yogurt cheese, and sour cream. This process for making crème fraîche, the French-style sour cream, is super simple, fun, and so much less expensive when you do it yourself. Look for pasteurized organic heavy cream that has not been ultra-pasteurized; the processing involved in ultra-pasteurization inhibits the reaction needed for culturing success. This is lovely served over a bowl of fresh berries, dolloped on pie in place of ice cream, or as a creamy accompaniment to smoked salmon with capers or the Beluga Lentil "Caviar" (*see* page 160). Use it wherever you might turn to sour cream and gussy it up with herbs or spices to create flavors.

1 cup heavy cream
  (**not ultra-pasteurized**)

1 tablespoon organic plain
  yogurt

Heat the cream in the microwave for 45 seconds or in a saucepan over low heat just until it reaches 90° to 95°F, 1 to 2 minutes if the cream was cold. Whisk in the yogurt. Pour the mixture into a sterile glass jar and secure the lid. Leave it at room temperature, shaking every 4 hours for 12 hours. Remove the lid. It should have thickened, should smell sweet and grassy, and have a slight tangy taste. It will thicken further in the fridge. Keep refrigerated and use within 1 week.

BLACK PEPPER CRÈME FRAÎCHE

Stir in 1 tablespoon freshly ground black pepper into 1 cup Home-Churned Crème Fraîche. **Makes 1 cup.**

LEMON-HERB CRÈME FRAÎCHE

Stir 1 teaspoon each freshly grated lemon zest, chopped fresh tarragon, and chopped fresh dill into 1 cup Home-Churned Crème Fraîche. **Makes 1 cup.**

SWEET CRÈME FRAÎCHE

Stir 1 ounce fortified, Rich Simple Syrup (*see* page 6) or honey into 1 cup Home-Churned Crème Fraîche. **Makes 1 cup.**

PICADILLO

MAKES ABOUT 4½ CUPS Picadillo is a savory ground meat hash. The word is derived from the Spanish *picar*, meaning "to finely chop." Many Spanish-speaking countries have a variation. Whether it's used as a filling for tacos or empanadas or eaten with rice and beans, it's delicious. I must say that sandwiched in a bun, it makes the best Sloppy Joe. This makes more than you'll need for the Warming Hut Board (*see* page 104). Serve half there and save the rest for omelets, burritos, taco salads, stuffed peppers, and more.

2 tablespoons vegetable oil

1 white onion, chopped

4 garlic cloves, minced

½ teaspoon kosher salt

½ teaspoon ground cinnamon

¼ teaspoon ground cumin

⅛ teaspoon ground nutmeg

⅛ teaspoon ground cloves

1 pound ground beef

2 to 3 jalapeños, seeded and finely diced

2 large ripe tomatoes, chopped

3 tablespoons red wine vinegar

2 tablespoons golden raisins

2 tablespoons toasted slivered almonds

¼ cup sliced manzanilla olives

1 tablespoon drained capers

Kosher salt

Freshly ground black pepper

Heat the oil in a large skillet over medium-high heat. Add the onion and garlic and cook until the onion softens, 8 to 10 minutes. Add the salt and spices to the pan and cook, stirring to incorporate, until the spices are aromatic and blended, about 1 minute.

Add the beef to the pan, breaking it up into fine crumbles as it browns. Add the jalapeños, tomatoes, and red wine vinegar. Cook, stirring, until most of the liquid has evaporated. Stir in the raisins, almonds, olives, and capers.

Reduce heat to low and cook for 5 minutes, stirring occasionally. Remove from heat, taste, and season with salt and pepper, as needed. Serve warm.

Crackers & Breads

Store-bought crackers and breads are easy to stock up or to have on hand, but sometimes you want to gussy them up a little, make your own from scratch, or refresh the odds and ends of the bread box in inventive ways. Every food board needs a crunchy vehicle for getting all the other goodies into your mouth, and the recipes that follow are a few fast, favorite ways to do just that.

BRAT TOTS

MAKES ABOUT 2½ DOZEN TOTS This is my two-bite American take on a British pub favorite—bangers and mash. Tasty tots dotted with sausage and deep fried are irresistible. Use a diced Bratwurst link or smoked sausage (I'm partial to the latter, but like the sound of Brat Tot)—it's a perfectly fitting recipe for the Village Pub Board (*see* page 22). Moisture is the enemy of a crispy tater tot, so you want to remove as much of it from the shredded potatoes as possible. The key to tater tots that hold their shape while frying is the freezing step. Enjoy these alone, with ketchup, or the Creamy Remoulade (*see* page 133).

3 russet potatoes (2 pounds), peeled

¼ pound bratwurst or smoked sausage, diced

2 tablespoons sliced chives

1 teaspoon garlic powder

2 teaspoons kosher salt

1 teaspoon freshly ground black pepper

1 cup all-purpose flour

Vegetable oil, for frying

Peel the potatoes and place in a saucepan with water to cover. Bring to a boil and cook for 5 to 7 minutes to partially cook; drain. When cool enough to handle, shred them on the large holes of a box grater or in a food processor fitted with the shredding disk.

Pile the shredded potatoes in the center of a clean flour sack kitchen towel or double layer of cheesecloth. Gather up the corners and tie and twist over the sink to extract as much liquid as possible from the potatoes.

Transfer the potatoes to a mixing bowl and add the diced sausage, chives, garlic powder, salt, pepper, and 1 tablespoon of the flour. Place the remaining flour on a plate and set aside. Mix the potato mixture well to combine. Form tablespoons of mixture into tots and arrange on a baking sheet lined with parchment paper. Freeze the formed tots for 30 minutes.

Heat the vegetable oil to 375°F in a cast-iron skillet. Remove the tots from the freezer and roll them in the flour on the plate to lightly coat. Carefully drop 7 to 8 tots in the oil at a time and do not disturb for 2 minutes. Gently roll over and cook on the second side. Remove with a slotted spoon and drain on paper towels. Continue until all the tots are cooked.

BACON-WRAPPED CRACKERS

MAKES 2 DOZEN   A half dozen years ago, I developed seventy-five new recipes for *Garden & Gun* magazine's first cookbook—*The Southerner's Cookbook*. Among them, I shared a recipe that the woman who became my grandmother-in-law served to me and my family on her well-appointed, screened-in porch over cocktails the first time we met some twenty-five years ago. Belts of bacon cinch the crackers as they bake, creating a savory silhouette. These are so simple to make and crazy delicious. Tuck a few fresh leaves of a woody herb like rosemary or thyme beneath the belt of bacon or sprinkle the bacon with a bit of brown sugar before baking, if desired.

6 thin bacon slices

24 saltine or butter crackers, or a mix of the two

Fresh rosemary or thyme leaves (optional)

Brown sugar (optional)

Preheat the oven to 275°F. Arrange a rack on a foil-lined baking sheet.

Stack the bacon strips and cut them in half crosswise with a chef's knife, and then cut each stack in half lengthwise so that you have 24 strips of bacon.

Place a cracker in the center of each bacon strip and bring the ends over the top of each cracker. Overlap to create a "belt" of bacon that will remain secure during baking.

Tuck a few rosemary or thyme leaves beneath each bacon belt, or add a pinch of brown sugar on top, if desired. Transfer the crackers to the rack set on the prepared baking sheet.

Bake for 1 hour. Cool to serve.

SMOKY CHEESE TWISTS

MAKES ABOUT 2 DOZEN The convenience of frozen pastry dough and the powdery Parmesan from a shaker canister cannot be understated because they make this addictive nibble a cinch to prepare. The powdery cheese acts like flour on the work surface when rolling the dough. Freshly grated Manchego adds a truffle-y, nutty flavor that I love. Use whatever cheese you like. These are best enjoyed while warm from the oven but can also be made ahead. Just prep and twist the dough, but don't bake. Freeze the dough twists on the pan for up to a few hours before baking. Then pop these in the oven when your guests arrive (just add 3 minutes to the baking time). Puff pastry dough makes these light and crispy, but you may also use bread dough, pizza dough, or crescent roll dough similarly.

½ cup grated Parmesan, such as Kraft

1 sheet frozen puff pastry dough, thawed

¾ cup finely grated Manchego

½ teaspoon smoked paprika

½ teaspoon kosher salt

2 tablespoons unsalted butter, melted

Preheat the oven to 400°F. Line a baking sheet with parchment paper.

Sprinkle ¼ cup of the Parmesan on a clean work surface and unfold the pastry sheet on top of the cheese.

Roll the dough a few times to press the dough into the cheese and work out the creases. Roll into a 12 x 12-inch square.

Sprinkle with the Manchego, ¼ teaspoon of the smoked paprika, and the salt. Fold the dough in half and roll gently to seal. Cut the dough crosswise with a pizza cutter or chef's knife into 24 (½-inch) strips. Brush the strips with the melted butter and sprinkle with the remaining ¼ cup Parmesan and ¼ teaspoon paprika.

Twist each strip tightly and transfer to the baking sheet, pressing the ends to the parchment to keep them from unrolling. Bake for 10 minutes until puffed up and golden. Remove from oven and turn the twists over; cook for 2 minutes more. Serve warm or cool completely on a wire rack and store in an airtight container in the refrigerator. Reheat on low in the oven to warm to serve.

ROSEMARY CORN MUFFINS

MAKES 1 DOZEN My mom was a muffin maker. Well, really, she was a first-grade teacher who made muffins all the time—blueberry muffins, lemon poppy-seed muffins, cinnamon muffins, and her "special" bran muffins with raisins that made me gag as a kid. Somewhere along the way her muffin making went mini. Gone were the big ones that swelled above paper liners, usurped by bready little bites that kept you going back for more. Her switch surely had us eating more than we did before. Mini corn muffins with sour cream were in her regular rotation. I've added fresh rosemary to the recipe. Serve these with Maple-Chipotle Butter (*see* page 141).

1 cup self-rising yellow cornmeal

½ cup all-purpose flour

½ cup sour cream

½ cup whole milk

1½ teaspoons minced fresh rosemary

1 teaspoon sugar

1 teaspoon kosher salt

1 large egg, beaten

2 tablespoons melted unsalted butter or rendered bacon fat

Place a mini muffin pan on the center rack of the oven. Preheat the oven to 400°F.

Combine the cornmeal and flour in a quart-size liquid measuring cup (*see* Tip below) or mixing bowl. Mix in the sour cream, milk, rosemary, sugar, salt, and egg with a wood spoon.

Remove the muffin pan from the oven. Add ½ teaspoon melted butter or bacon fat to each muffin cup. Divide the batter evenly between each cup.

Bake at 400°F until lightly browned, 10 to 12 minutes. Invert onto a wire rack. Cool completely, about 15 minutes.

TIP: Mixing the batter in a large liquid measuring cup makes pouring it into the muffin pan easier.

BAGEL CHIPS

MAKES ABOUT 8 SERVINGS   This almost isn't a recipe it's so easy. My kids love bagels, but inevitably we end up with a few ignored ones at the bottom of a bag. I started slicing them super thin, spraying them with a bit of olive oil cooking spray, and toasting them in the oven for bagel chips. I keep them sealed in an airtight tin in the pantry. They're perfect for food boards. You can do this with any type of bagel. I slice whole bagels into thin rounds and pieces, and pre-sliced bagel halves into any which way I can finagle it. It doesn't matter. Chips come in all sizes.

4 stale or fresh bagels of any kind

Olive oil cooking spray

Optional seasonings: poppy seeds, sesame seeds, dried onion, cinnamon-sugar, everything-bagel seasoning, grated asiago, grated parmesan

Preheat the oven to 300°F. Line a baking sheet with parchment paper.

Cut a small slice off the bottom of a whole bagel to create a flat surface that will keep the bagel steady as you slice. Slice into thin ⅛- to ¼-inch slices. For bagel halves, slice thinly crosswise into narrow pieces.

Arrange the slices in a single layer on the baking sheet and spray generously with the olive oil. Top with any of the optional seasonings, if desired. Spray again. Turn each piece over and spray the second side, seasoning and spraying again, if desired. (Spraying the seasonings after sprinkling helps them adhere). Bake for 15 to 20 minutes until golden brown and crisp.

NOTE: You do not have to use day-old or stale bagels, but I find that they are easier to slice thinly when they're a bit firmer, plus they crisp up faster in the oven. You also do not have to use standard bagel seasonings. Try gochugaru Korean chile flakes (*see* page 16) or Tajín seasoning to reinvent the wheel (heh heh!).

Snacks & Nibbles

Happy hour is always better with a substantial bite or two to buffer
the effects of imbibing, but also to complement the cocktail. I have
a salty tooth, so I tend to whip up nibbles that satisfy that craving.
The recipes that follow are tried-and-true go-tos. Many are fresh
takes on the retro nibbles that I grew up eating, while others are
inspired by travels or a fun food board theme.

REUBENS-IN-A-BLANKET

MAKES 2 DOZEN Make refrigerated bread dough taste like rye with a sprinkle of crushed caraway seeds. A rolling pin makes easy work of crushing seeds or spices, which helps release more flavor. Other conveniences make this nibble a cinch to pull together—sliced meat and cheese from the deli, jarred kraut, and even bottled dressing. If you can't find bottled Russian dressing, it's super easy to make from ingredients you likely have on hand (see page 135).

1 (11-ounce) package refrigerated breadstick dough

¾ pound sliced corned beef

2 slices Swiss cheese

2 tablespoons caraway seeds, crushed

¼ cup drained sauerkraut

½ cup plus 2 tablespoons Russian Dressing (see page 135)

3 tablespoons melted salted butter

Preheat the oven to 375°F. Line a baking sheet with parchment paper.

Open the canister of breadstick dough and unroll the dough. The dough will be scored to easily divide into 12 strips. Cut crosswise through the strips with a chef's knife so that you have 24 (3-inch) strips of dough.

Divide the corned beef slices into 2 even stacks. Cut each stack into 12 equal portions. Cut each slice of Swiss cheese into 12 equal portions. Arrange a dough strip on a work surface and sprinkle the dough with a pinch of crushed caraway seeds. Place a stacked corned beef portion in the center of the dough. Top with a piece of the cheese, ½ teaspoon of the sauerkraut, and ¼ teaspoon of the Russian dressing. Bring the ends of the dough up and over the filling and crimp together to secure before placing on the prepared baking sheet, spacing them 1 inch apart. Brush the tops with melted butter and sprinkle each with another pinch of crushed caraway seeds.

Bake in the oven for about 12 minutes until the bread is golden brown and the cheese is melted.

WEST INDIES SALAD

MAKES ABOUT 2 CUPS I have lots of favorite cocktail-hour nibbles, but this may be tops. It is so simple to make and always gets rave reviews. I'll willingly admit that I've been caught taking a sip or two of the marinade once all the crab has been eaten. This is an eighty-year-old Southern classic. Purists will tell you that it ain't West Indies Salad unless it's made with Wesson oil, but I've made it with avocado and olive oil (not extra-virgin) with delicious results.

2 teaspoons kosher salt

1 teaspoon freshly ground black pepper

1 teaspoon lemon zest

1 cup finely chopped yellow onion

1 pound lump crabmeat, picked of shell

½ cup apple cider vinegar

½ cup vegetable oil

Crackers

6 to 8 lemon wedges

Combine the salt, pepper, and zest in a small bowl.

Layer ½ cup of the onion in a shallow dish. Top with the crabmeat. Sprinkle the seasoning mixture over the crab. Cover the crabmeat with the remaining ½ cup onion.

Pour the vinegar and oil over everything. Cover the dish with plastic wrap and refrigerate for at least 4 hours or up to 12 hours.

Serve with crackers and the lemon wedges.

BUYING CRAB
Crabmeat is cooked—steamed or boiled—before it is picked and packed. If it fits your budget, buy fresh, just-picked unpasteurized crabmeat that is packed on ice, keep it chilled, and use within 3 days. These are all your buying options in order of fancy to frugal:

FRESH CRABMEAT
Jumbo Lump Crabmeat: The sweet tender nuggets of meat comprise this luxe option that comes from the swimmer fins. Since each crab only has two, it takes meat from a lot of crabs to make a pound.

Lump Crabmeat: These large, sturdy flakes of sweet crabmeat come from the body of the crab and hold their shape in recipes.

Backfin Crabmeat: Buy this small flake crabmeat that comes from the body and back of the crab for crab cakes or other recipes where a fine flake is fitting.

Crab Claw Meat: These economical large, dark nuggets come from the front claw and have a pronounced crab flavor that shines through when mixed with other ingredients.

Flake or Special Crabmeat: This is a mix of odd bits and different textures.

CANNED CRABMEAT
Pasteurized Crabmeat: Heated to kill bacteria and extend shelf life, this comes frozen, in cans, or in plastic tubs that must remain refrigerated. Canned is my least favorite. It can have funky off-flavors. Plastic containers are better, but frozen is best in my book.

Shelf-Stable Crabmeat: This has been heated the longest for packaging and is an altogether different beast that is shelf stable for 18 months or indefinitely, but does not compare to fresh crabmeat.

CAJUN CHICKEN POPS

SERVES 4 TO 6 AS AN APPETIZER (ABOUT 3 WINGS PER PERSON) Chicken wings have three sections: the pointy tip, the flat wingette, and the meaty drumette that looks like a mini drumstick. You want drumettes for this recipe. These are tantalizingly spicy and really demand a creamy, cooling sauce. The Creamy Remoulade (*see* page 133) is an ideal one for dunking these chicken pops.

½ **cup Louisiana brand hot sauce**

1 **stick unsalted butter**

20 **chicken drumettes**

1½ **tablespoons Cajun seasoning**

1½ **teaspoon kosher salt**

½ **teaspoon dried oregano**

½ **teaspoon cayenne**

Creamy Remoulade (*see* **page 133)**

Position an oven rack in the top position and preheat the broiler. Line a baking pan with aluminum foil and spray with cooking spray.

Combine the hot sauce and butter in a small saucepan over medium-high heat. Cook, whisking, until the butter is melted and incorporated. Set aside and keep warm.

Pat the drumettes dry with paper towels and place them in a large bowl. Combine the Cajun seasoning, salt, oregano, and cayenne in a small bowl. Sprinkle the chicken with the seasoning blend and toss to coat. Arrange the seasoned chicken on the prepared baking sheet. Broil until the drumettes are browned and crispy, 15 minutes. Turn and broil for 10 minutes more.

Remove the pan from the oven and brush the chicken with the hot sauce mixture. Return to the oven to cook for 3 minutes. Remove the pan, turn the chicken over, and brush with more hot sauce mixture. Cook for 3 minutes more. Remove and serve immediately.

TOMATO, MELON & FETA SKEWERS

SERVES 6 Skewers on a food board are easy to pick up and so simple to make, plus they are a great way to add color and interest. Thread veggies and fruit, such as berries or melon balls, with cubes of cheese or meat, olives, pickles, or even cooked filled pasta like cheese-stuffed tortellini or ravioli. The only limit is your imagination. I love a watermelon and tomato salad in summertime—ingredients that work perfectly for a skewered salad with salty feta. Instead of a vinaigrette, a drizzle of basil oil adds color and flavor. Blanching the leaves mere seconds and then shocking in ice water locks in the bright green color.

2½ cups packed basil leaves

1 cup extra virgin olive oil

¼ teaspoon kosher salt

1½ cups cubed watermelon (1-inch cubes)

1 cup cubed feta (1½-inch cubes)

Red or yellow grape tomatoes

18 small basil leaves

Freshly ground black pepper

Prepare an ice bath and set aside. Bring a medium saucepan to a rolling boil. Add the basil and cook for 10 to 15 seconds. Drain and plunge the basil into the ice water to rapidly chill. Drain again and squeeze of excess moisture.

Put the blanched basil in a blender with the olive oil and salt. Blend until smooth. Set the blender pitcher aside for 1 hour to allow the solids and foam to settle. Strain through a cheesecloth-lined strainer. Use immediately or refrigerate for up to 3 days until ready to use. Bring to room temperature before serving.

Thread 18 (4-inch) skewers with the watermelon, feta, and tomatoes. The order or pattern doesn't matter. Finish with a small basil leaf. Arrange on a food board or platter and drizzle with the basil oil. Sprinkle with pepper.

NOTE: Herb and garlic oils are notorious for harboring the bacteria that causes botulism—not the Botox you want to mess around with. Blanching helps kill any bacteria on the leaves but doesn't keep any new bacteria from growing once it's blended into oil. To be safe, use this within 3 days and keep refrigerated when not in use. Or use the ice cube method: Pour the oil into an ice tray and freeze it for up to 6 months. Pop out the cubes and store in a sealed freezer bag. Thaw what you need—each cube is 1 tablespoon—for an easy pop of summertime flavor anytime.

STEAMED BABY ARTICHOKES

SERVES 4 Serving artichokes always feels like a special occasion to me. As a kid we couldn't scrape the leaves with our teeth fast enough to uncover the heart. Once we did, we'd always fight over it. When I lived in California, I was always awestruck when we drove past the fields of artichokes in Half Moon Bay. I stopped at any farm stand selling them and loved to get the almost completely edible baby ones. Grocery stores typically sell small ones that still require some serious prep work, but the tasty payoff is worth it. Serve these with Brown Butter Bagna Cauda (*see* page 136).

1 large lemon
1 pound baby artichokes

Fill a large pot with just enough water to touch the bottom of a steamer basket and bring to a boil.

Meanwhile, fill a large bowl with cold water. Cut the lemon in half. Squeeze the juice of half of the lemon into the water to acidulate and set the bowl aside.

Slice the top quarter off each artichoke using a serrated knife. Remove the most outer leaves. Cut the artichokes in half lengthwise and remove any hairy choke. As you work, rub all the cut surfaces of each artichoke with the second lemon half and then drop them in the acidulated water to prevent browning.

Drain the artichokes and transfer to the steamer basket. Cover the pot and steam until tender, 15 to 20 minutes. Remove and keep warm to serve.

SPAM MUSUBI

SERVES 4 TO 6 On my honeymoon in Kawaii, I ate a lot of musubi—the Spam-topped thumbs of rice wrapped in a nori seaweed belt. It's surprisingly addictive. Long before prepared sushi was available in almost every grocery store in America, gas stations and roadside stops all over Hawaii were offering up this humble two-bite treat that wraps the beloved potted meat like a gift for devouring. This recipe is fun to make and a great marriage of pantry ingredients, plus you can use the Spam can to mold the rice.

3 cups short-grain rice, such as Calrose

1 (12-ounce can) Spam

2 tablespoons brown sugar

2 tablespoons shoyu sauce

2 tablespoons mirin

Nori sheets, cut into ¼-inch strips

Furikake seasoning (optional)

Cook the rice according to the package instructions and keep warm.

Open the can of Spam and remove the meat and set aside. Use the can opener or kitchen shears to cut open and remove the bottom of the can to create a Spam-shaped musubi mold. Wash it well with soapy water. Be careful not to cut yourself on any sharp edges.

Cut the block of Spam crosswise (from top to bottom) into 10 slices that are about ¼-inch thick. Combine the brown sugar, shoyu, and mirin in a large skillet and bring to a boil. Add the Spam and cook until crusty and caramelized, 5 to 6 minutes, turning halfway through. Remove the pan from heat and keep warm.

Set the hollow Spam can on a clean surface. Holding it steady, press the cooked rice into the can using the back of a spoon to create a brick of rice. Press the brick through, lifting the can away. Repeat with the remaining rice to create another brick. With a sharp chef's knife, slice each brick of rice crosswise (from top to bottom) into 5 slices that are about ½-inch thick. Wipe the blade of the knife clean after each cut for clean slices.

Place a slice of rice on a work surface. Top with a piece of the warm Spam. Cut in half crosswise so you have 2 bite-size pieces. Wrap a strip of nori around each square of rice and Spam and secure by gluing the wrapper to itself using a grain of the cooked sticky rice. Arrange the musubi on a platter and sprinkle with furikake seasoning, if desired.

SNEAKY CHEAT

If you don't have Spam, you can make this with thick slices of bologna or go vegan with teriyaki-marinated tofu.

ISLAND RUMAKI

MAKES 14 TO 16 Like the Bacon-Wrapped Crackers (*see page 146*), this is another retro bacon-wrapped appetizer that deserves to be in the limelight again. Canned water chestnuts are a crisp stand-in for the chicken livers used in classic rumaki and hold up well during cooking. Look for tender, young ginger root, which is easy to "mince" by rubbing a peeled piece against the holes of a fine grater.

¼ cup soy sauce

1½ tablespoons balsamic vinegar

2 teaspoons honey

3 tablespoons minced fresh ginger root

2 teaspoons Jamaican jerk seasoning

½ teaspoon cayenne

3 teaspoons grated lime zest

½ pound hickory-smoked bacon (not thick-cut)

1 (8-ounce) can whole water chestnuts, drained and rinsed

1 tablespoon chopped fresh cilantro or basil (optional)

Combine the soy sauce, balsamic vinegar, honey, ginger, jerk seasoning, cayenne, and lime zest in a bowl and whisk to combine.

Cut each piece of bacon crosswise into 2 pieces. Wrap a piece tightly around each water chestnut, securing with a toothpick. Arrange in a single layer in a small shallow dish. Pour the marinade evenly over the rumaki and brush to coat. Refrigerate for at least 2 hours.

Preheat the oven to 350°F. Cover a baking sheet with aluminum foil and spray it with cooking spray. Arrange the marinated rumaki about 1 inch apart on the pan. Bake until the bacon is crisp, 12 to 15 minutes. Sprinkle with the cilantro or basil before serving.

NOTE: This recipe may also be made using peeled, cubed sunchokes (also called Jerusalem artichokes) or jicama in place of the water chestnuts, though the finished result will not have the same crunch as water chestnuts.

SPICY PICKAPEPPA NUTS

MAKES ABOUT 3 CUPS My grandmother loved to make seasoned nuts. She candied them with a glaze of honey, "smoked" them with a soak in liquid smoke, or bathed them in butter and toasted them with an array of spices and rubs. A bowlful was always on the coffee table when drinks were served, and her latest batch regularly showed up in small packages in my mailbox at college with punny little notes tucked inside that read "Believe it or nut, I love you!" or "Cannut wait to see you!" While this isn't her recipe, it is her soak-and-roast method. I usually make sweet-and-savory Pickapeppa pecans, but since that unique condiment hails from Jamaica, it seems a perfectly fitting treatment for tropical macadamias on the Tiki Bar Board (*see page 84*), but use whatever nut you love.

8 ounces raw nuts

¼ cup plus 1 tablespoon Pickapeppa Sauce

2 tablespoons pineapple juice

2 tablespoons dark brown sugar

1½ teaspoons kosher salt

¼ teaspoon cayenne pepper

Place the nuts in a sandwich bag, seal, and set aside.

Whisk together the Pickapeppa Sauce, pineapple juice, dark brown sugar, salt, and cayenne in a small bowl until the sugar is dissolved. Pour over the nuts, squeeze out the air from the bag, and seal. Shake gently to make sure all the nuts are coated with the sauce. Set aside for at least 4 hours, shaking from time to time or refrigerate overnight to allow the nuts to absorb the flavors.

Preheat the oven to 350°F. Strain the nuts of excess liquid and spread the nuts out in a single layer on a parchment-lined baking sheet. Bake for 15 minutes, shaking the pan halfway through, until the nuts are fragrant and tacky. Remove from the oven and transfer to a plate to cool completely. They will dry and crisp as they cool.

PANTRY GEM

Pickapeppa Sauce is a mainstay in my house for the fast-and-easy bold flavor it lends to everything. The distinctive Jamaican sauce has been produced for over one hundred years and is an integral player in "jerked" meats. It is composed of tomatoes, onion, chiles, vinegar, mangoes, raisins, and spices, and can be used as a condiment, marinade, baste, or cocktail mixer—it's a tasty swap for Worcestershire sauce in a Bloody Mary.

WARM OLIVE MEDLEY

MAKES 2 CUPS   It doesn't get much easier than this. Whether you get your olives from the olive bar at the grocery store or from jars in your pantry, rinse them well before you prepare this recipe, otherwise the varied brines and seasonings may collide with lackluster results. For the chile pepper, I use the no-name red chiles in the jar labeled "red chile peppers" in the spice aisle. I have always wondered what kind they are.

1½ cups mixed olives, pitted or with pits

1½ tablespoons extra-virgin olive oil

2 lemon peel strips

2 orange peel strips

1 bay leaf

1 fresh thyme sprig

¼ cup red sweety drops peppers (*see* Pantry Gem *right*)

¼ cup Marcona almonds

Put the olives in a strainer and rinse well under running water. Drain and pat dry.

Heat the olive oil in a large skillet over low heat. Add the olives, lemon and orange peels, bay leaf, thyme sprig, peppers, and almonds, and cook to gently warm through, about 10 minutes. Transfer to a warm serving bowl.

PANTRY GEM
Peruvian sweety drops peppers are a staple of olive bars these days alongside the bigger peppadews. These teardrop-shaped, mild pickled peppers come in cans or jars and are a great pantry staple that add a bright spot to a relish tray, salad, or skewer.

BELUGA LENTIL "CAVIAR"

MAKES ABOUT 2 CUPS   I created this recipe for glistening beluga lentil caviar for a vendor to pass out at San Francisco's Fancy Food Show many years ago, and then shared it in the final issue of *Cottage Living* magazine a few years later. It's an inexpensive vegetarian nod to the luxe real thing, but it's equally elegant. For fun, serve this as you would caviar. The lentils and shallots can be made up several days in advance.

¾ cup Beluga lentils, sorted and rinsed

1 bay leaf

1 fresh thyme sprig

1½ cups chicken stock

4 tablespoons sherry vinegar

1 tablespoon freshly squeezed lemon juice

1 teaspoon kosher salt

½ teaspoon freshly ground black pepper

2 tablespoons cup extra-virgin olive oil

1 tablespoon Agrumato lemon oil or lemon-infused oil

2 tablespoons unsalted butter

3 medium shallots, peeled and thinly sliced

1 teaspoon kosher salt

3 tablespoons crème de cassis

1 cup sour cream

¼ cup snipped fresh chives

Bagel Chips (*see* page 149)

Combine the lentils, bay leaf, thyme, and stock in a large saucepan and bring to a boil. Reduce heat to simmer and cover. Cook, stirring occasionally, until tender, 20 to 30 minutes. Drain. Transfer the lentils to a bowl and cool to room temperature.

Meanwhile, whisk 2 tablespoons of the sherry vinegar with the lemon juice, salt, and pepper in a small bowl. Gradually whisk in the olive and lemon oils until emulsified. Pour the dressing over the cooled lentils, taste, and adjust the seasoning, if needed, then set aside or refrigerate up to a few days.

Melt the butter in a large sauté pan. Add the shallots and salt and sauté over low heat until soft and caramelized, about 30 minutes. Transfer the shallots to a bowl and return the pan to the stove over medium-high heat. Add the remaining 2 tablespoons sherry vinegar and stir for 30 seconds to deglaze the pan. Immediately, pour the hot vinegar into the bowl with the shallots and add the crème de cassis. Stir to incorporate. Let the shallot mixture cool.

Arrange the lentils, shallots, sour cream, and chives in small bowls on a platter with a basket of potato chips. To eat, top a chip with a spoonful of lentils, a tangle of shallots, sour cream, and snipped chives.

STUFFED MUSHROOMS

SERVES 6 My grandmother, Eunice, was one of the finest cooks I've known. A meal in her Temple, Texas, home always began with cocktail hour—usually bourbon-and-something (if only an ice cube) in a glass and lots of savory appetizers. She was famous for her "Texas Trash," a cereal, nut, and cracker mix that she bathed in melted butter before baking; hickory-smoked pecans made from new-crop Texas nuts; and rich stuffed mushrooms. I've created variations on her mushroom recipe for years, and it remains a steadfast favorite party appetizer.

40 small cremini or white mushrooms, stems removed

1 (1.75-ounce) jar or ⅓ cup pine nuts, toasted

1 cup loosely packed fresh flat-leaf parsley leaves

1 cup loosely packed fresh basil leaves

½ cup grated Parmigiano-Reggiano

Zest of 1 lemon

Juice of 1 lemon

½ teaspoon kosher salt

¼ teaspoon cayenne

1 garlic clove, minced

2 tablespoons olive oil

Heat a large dry skillet over medium-high heat. Arrange the mushroom caps, hollow side up, in the pan and cook for 5 minutes, shaking the pan from time to time. Turn the caps over and cook for 5 minutes more, shaking occasionally. Remove from heat and place the mushrooms, stem sides down, on paper towels to drain and cool.

Place ¼ cup of the pine nuts in a food processor fitted with the metal blade; reserve the remaining pine nuts for garnish. Add the parsley, basil, Parmigiano, lemon zest and juice, salt, cayenne, and garlic and process until finely chopped. Slowly pour the oil through the food tube until incorporated.

Turn the mushrooms over and fill each cap with a mounded teaspoon of the pesto. Garnish each evenly with the reserved pine nuts.

SNEAKY CHEAT

Pesto is easy to make, but it's also easy to buy in jars to have on hand when summertime is a distant memory. Buitoni Pesto is a fresh-tasting, refrigerated brand that is preservative-free. Jarred pesto can be super oily or have funky flavors, so it's worth knowing which ones you like. When you don't have time to make your own, stuff these mushrooms with a prepared pesto of your choosing. Just taste it first and tweak the seasoning if it needs it—a bit more garlic, a hit of acid from vinegar or lemon, and perhaps more grated Parmigiano if it seems runny.

Sources

BOOKS

Jerry Thomas Bartenders Guide,
Jerry Thomas (1862)

*The American Bar: The Artistry of
Mixing Drinks,* Charles Schumann (1995)

*D.I.Y. Delicious: Recipes and Ideas for
Simple Food from Scratch,* Vanessa Barrington
(2010)

The Drunken Botanist, Amy Stewart (2013)

Meehan's Bartender Manual, Jim Meehan
(2017)

*The Cocktail Garden: Botanical Cocktails
for Every Season,* Ed Loveday (2017)

*The Spirit of the North: Cocktail Recipes
and Stories from Scandinavia,* Selma Slabiak
(2018)

WEBSITES

alcademics.com

supercall.com

mrbostondrinks.com

talesofthecocktails.com

diffordsguide.com

punchdrink.com

culinarylore.com

eater.com

cocktailsandbars.com

Acknowledgments

Much gratitude to the Tiller Press team for the opportunity to produce my third cookbook for Simon & Schuster. Special thanks to my editor, Anja Schmidt; senior designer Matt Ryan, who went above and beyond by re-creating each food board in this book with a food stylist's eye for the illustrator; creative director Patrick Sullivan; publisher Theresa DiMasi; editorial assistant Samantha Lubash; and PR/Marketing pros Lauren Ollerhead, Laura Flavin, Molly Pieper, and Sam Ford for all you do to make sure each book happens, looks great, and gets into the hands of readers.

To my many Blueline Creative Group partners, including recipe testers on this book, Rebecca Withers and Carlos Briceño, I have enjoyed our collaborations immensely and look forward to more reasons to drink and eat under the guise of work. To my talented friend, Maya Metz Logue, who painstakingly illustrated the cocktails, ingredients, and food boards in this book. Your artistry blows my mind and elevates my words and recipes, and I'm beyond honored that you agreed to illustrate this book.

To everyone reading this, I eagerly look forward to the day maskless merrymaking safely resumes. Clink, clink to friends, family, food, fellowship, and the brighter future that surely awaits!

Index